RELATIC

Becoming a Caring Community

General Editor
LYMAN COLEMAN

Managing Editor
DENISE BELTZNER

Assistant Editors
DOUGLAS LaBUDDE
KEITH MADSEN
STEPHEN SHEELY

Cover Art
CHRISTOPHER WERNER

Cover Design
ERIKA TIEPEL

Layout Production
FRONTLINE GROUP
SHARON PENINGTON

Seven Stages to Building Healthy Relationships

SESSION	ENTRY LEVEL	ADVANCED LEVEL
1 ORIENTATION	Getting Down to the Basics Genesis 2:18–25	
2 LOVING GOD	The Greatest Commandment Mark 12:28–34	Resisting Satan James 4:1–10
3 LOVING OURSELVES	Realizing Our Potential Mark 14:27–31, 66–72	Children of God 1 John 2:28–3:3
4 LOVING FAMILY	A Family Conflict Luke 15:11–32	Family Relations Ephesians 5:22–6:4
5 LOVING OTHERS: INSIDE THE COMMUNITY OF FAITH	A Life of Service John 13:2–17	Stretching Our Boundaries Acts 10:9–23
6 LOVING OTHERS: OUTSIDE THE COMMUNITY OF FAITH	Breaking Barriers John 4:4–26	Loving Outsiders Romans 12:9–21
7 LOVING OUR ENEMIES	Some People Matthew 5:38–48	Paul's Enemies Philippians 1:12–18a, 27–2:4

Serendipity House / Box 1012 / Littleton, CO 80160
1-800-525-9563 / www.serendipityhouse.com
97 98 99 / **201F series•CHG** / 4 3 2 1

ACKNOWLEDGMENTS

To Zondervan Bible Publishers
for permission to use
the NIV text,
The Holy Bible, New International Bible Society.
© 1973, 1978, 1984 by International Bible Society.
Used by permission of Zondervan Bible Publishers

Instructions for Group Leader

PURPOSE: **What is this course all about?** This course allows you to deal with relationships in a supportive group relationship.

SEEKERS/ STRUGGLERS: **Who is this course designed for?** Two kinds of people: (a) Seekers who do not know where they are with God but are open to finding out, and (b) Strugglers who are committed to Jesus Christ, and want to grow in their faith.

NEW PEOPLE: **Does this mean I can invite my non-church friends?** Absolutely. In fact, this would be a good place for people on their way back to God to start.

STUDY: **What are we going to study?** Seven stages to building healthy relationships with various people (see Table of Contents), and Biblical strategies for strengthening these relationships.

FIRST SESSION: **What do we do at the meetings?** In the first session you get acquainted and decide on the Ground Rules for your group. In sessions two through seven, you have two options for Bible study.

TWO OPTIONS: **What are the two options?** OPTION 1—This study is best for newly formed groups or groups that are unfamiliar with small group Bible study. This option primarily contains multiple-choice questions, with no right or wrong answers.

OPTION 2—This study is best for groups who have had previous small group Bible studies and want to dig deeper into the Scriptures. Option 2 questions are deeper—and the Scripture is a teaching passage.

CHOOSING AN OPTION: **Which option of Bible study do you recommend?** The OPTION 1 study is best for newly formed groups, groups that are unfamiliar with small group Bible study, or groups that are only meeting for an hour. The OPTION 2 study is best for deeper Bible study groups, or groups which meet for more than an hour.

CHOOSING BOTH OPTIONS:	**Can we choose both options?** If your group meets for 90 to 120 minutes, you can choose to do both studies at the same time. Or you can spend two weeks on a unit—OPTION 1 the first week and OPTION 2 the next. Or you can do one of the options in the meeting and the other option for homework.
SMALL GROUP:	**What's different about this course?** It is written for a small group to do together.
GROUP BUILDING:	**What is the purpose behind your approach to Bible study?** To give everyone a chance to share their own "spiritual story," and to bond as a group. This is often referred to as "koinonia."
KOINONIA:	**What is koinonia and why is it a part of these studies?** Koinonia means "fellowship." It is an important part of these sessions, because as a group gets to know one another, they are more willing to share their needs and care for one another.
BIBLE KNOWLEDGE:	**What if I don't know much about the Bible?** No problem. Option 1 is based on a Bible story that stands on its own—to discuss as though you were hearing it for the first time. Both options often come with Comments —to keep you up to speed.
COMMENTS:	**What is the purpose of the Comments in the studies?** To help you understand the context of the Bible passage or to assist you in further reflection on how this passage relates to your life.
LEADERSHIP:	**Who leads the meetings?** Ideally, there should be three people: (a) trained leader, (b) apprentice or co-leader, and (c) host. Having an apprentice-in-training in the group, you have a built-in system for multiplying the group if it gets too large. In fact, this is one of the goals of the group—to give "birth" to a new group in time.

Beginning a Small Group

1. AGENDA: There are three parts to every group meeting.

GATHERING	BIBLE STUDY	CARING TIME
15 min.	30 min.	15–45 min.
Purpose:	Purpose:	Purpose:
To break the ice	To share your spiritual journey	To share prayer requests

2. FEARLESS FOURSOME: If you have more than 7 in your group at any time, call the option play when the time comes for Bible study, and subdivide into groups of 4 for greater participation. (In 4s, everyone will share and you can finish the Bible study in 30 minutes.) Then regather the group for the CARING TIME.

GATHERING	BIBLE STUDY	CARING TIME
All Together	Groups of 4	Back Together

3. EMPTY CHAIR: Pull up an empty chair during the CARING TIME at the close and ask God to fill this chair each week. Remember, by breaking into groups of 4 for the Bible study time, you can grow numerically without feeling "too big" as a group.

The Group Leader needs an apprentice-in-training at all times so that the apprentice can start a new "cell" when the group size is 12 or more.

SESSION 1
Orientation

PURPOSE

To get acquainted, to share your expectations, and to decide on the ground rules for your group.

AGENDA

 **Gathering**   **Bible Study**   **Caring Time**

OPEN

 ## GATHERING / 15 Minutes / All Together

Leader: The purpose of the Gathering time is to break the ice. Read the instructions for Step One and go first. Then read the Introduction (Step Two) and the instructions for the Bible Study.

Step One: Let Me Tell You About My Day ... What was your day like today? Or your week? Month? Year? Choose one of the items below to help you describe your day to the group. Feel free to elaborate, but allow enough time for each group member to share.

❏ a Greek tragedy   ❏ a soap opera
❏ a fairy tale   ❏ the late night news
❏ a Clint Eastwood movie   ❏ a pro wrestling match
❏ a Bible epic   ❏ a boring lecture
❏ a fireworks display   ❏ a rainy spring day
❏ an episode of *The Three Stooges*

INTRODUCTION

Step Two: Welcome. Welcome to this course on building better relationships. In this session, we will get an overview of what we will study for these seven sessions. Relationships form the foundation of who we are and how we relate to the world around us. Without relationships, life would be uninteresting and dehumanizing. Through our relationships, we learn what it means to be a created human being.

Dr. Theodore Rubin in his book, *One to One: Understanding Personal Relationships*, writes the following about relationships:

We are relating beings. Indeed, for our species we may almost say that to be is to relate. From the earliest times in our lives, we develop and sustain feelings about ourselves and other people. Sometimes we are in touch with these feelings. Sometimes we distort them, and there are times we are not in touch with them at all. There are also times when we share what we feel about ourselves and one another. These feelings, and the way we share them (or don't share them), determine the nature of our relationships.

But relationships are not automatically great. Successful relationships with God and with others take work in order to be healthy and strong. They do not just happen. At the center of successful relationships is love and respect. Healthy relationships are marked by equality—equal giving and receiving—or else you will find yourself in a co-dependent relationship. Healthy relationships are balanced ones and they add to our lives. Unhealthy relationships throw our lives off-balance.

In these sessions, we will look at some of our relationships with others. We will consider our need for relationships, our relationship with God, with ourselves, with family members, with others (both "in and out" of the community of faith), and with our enemies. By examining these relationships, we will discover the important components of relationships and gain skills for developing healthy relationships.

THREE PARTS TO A SESSION

Every session has three parts: (1) **Gathering**—to break the ice and introduce the topic, (2) **Bible Study**—to share your own study through a passage of Scripture, and (3) **Caring Time**—to decide what action you need to take in this area of your life and to support one another in this action.

In this course, the Bible Study approach is a little unique with a different focus. Usually, the content of the passage is the focus of the Bible Study. In this course, the focus will be on telling your "story," using the passage as a springboard.

 # BIBLE STUDY / 30 Minutes / Groups of 4

Leader: If you have more than 7 in this session, we recommend groups of 4—4 to sit around the dining table, 4 around the kitchen table, and 4 around a folding table. Ask one person in each foursome to be the Leader and to complete the Bible Study in the time allowed. Then regather for the Caring Time, allowing 15–45 minutes.

STUDY

Read Genesis 2:18–25, and discuss the questions which follow with your group. This passage, which is part of the story of Creation, is where all relationships began. In each foursome, ask someone to be the Leader. Go around on the first question. Then go around on the next question, working through the questionnaire. After 30 minutes, the leader will call time and ask you to regather for the Caring Time.

¹⁸The Lord God said, "It is not good for man to be alone. I will make a suitable helper for him."

¹⁹Now the Lord God had formed out of the ground all the beasts of the field and all the birds of the air. He brought them to the man to see what he would name them; and whatever the man called each living creature, that was its name. ²⁰So the man gave names to all the livestock, the birds of the air and all the beasts of the field.

But for Adam no suitable helper was found. ²¹So the Lord God caused the man to fall into a deep sleep; and while he was sleeping, he took one of man's ribs and closed up the place with flesh. ²²Then the Lord God made a woman from the rib he had taken out of the man, and he brought her to the man.

²³The man said,

> "This is now bone of my bones
> and flesh of my flesh;
> she shall be called 'woman,'
> for she was taken out of man."

²⁴For this reason a man will leave his father and mother and be united to his wife, and they will become one flesh.

²⁵The man and his wife were both naked, and they felt no shame.

Genesis 2:18–25, NIV

1. Imagine that you were going to make a movie of this story in the Bible. Who might you want to cast in the role of Adam? Who would you cast as Eve? Choose from the lists below:

"What makes a person significant is not a gift like prophecy or knowledge, but the ability to love."
—Author unknown

ADAM
- ❐ Tom Cruise
- ❐ Lou Diamond Phillips
- ❐ Dustin Hoffman
- ❐ Fabio
- ❐ Denzel Washington

- ❐ Patrick Swayze
- ❐ Richard Gere
- ❐ Sidney Poitier
- ❐ Robin Williams
- ❐ Michael Douglas

EVE
- ❐ Julia Roberts
- ❐ Connie Sellecca
- ❐ Rhea Perlman
- ❐ Meryl Streep
- ❐ Bridget Fonda

- ❐ Whoopi Goldberg
- ❐ Meg Ryan
- ❐ Whitney Houston
- ❐ Roseanne
- ❐ Shelley Long

2. In promoting this movie, which of the following themes would you emphasize in your advertising?
   ❏ a romantic theme—the first man and woman exploring first love
   ❏ a theme of innocence—a time before drugs, greed and crime
   ❏ an ecological theme—when all of creation was at one with each other
   ❏ a family adventure theme—like Swiss Family Robinson

3. Where was your "Garden of Eden" as a child—the place you went to where everything seemed peaceful and harmonious?
   ❏ my room   ❏ my grandparents' home
   ❏ my church   ❏ a secret hideaway
   ❏ a friend's house   ❏ I didn't have such a place.
   ❏ a special place outside   ❏ other: _____

"We are born helpless. As soon as we are fully conscious we discover loneliness. We need others physically, emo- tionally, intellec- tually, we need them if we are to know anything, even ourselves."
—C. S. Lewis

4. Why do you think Adam could not find an animal to be a suitable companion and helper?
   ❏ It's hard to cuddle with a rhinoceros.
   ❏ They could not relate as equals.
   ❏ They were not "one flesh" with him.
   ❏ Animals are "too accepting"—they don't challenge you.
   ❏ I don't have any idea, since men also communicate in grunts.

5. What are the implications of the fact that the woman was taken out of the man?
   ❏ Women owe their existence to men.
   ❏ Women and men are part of the same thing and need each other to be whole.
   ❏ It's like the old saying—woman was not made out of man's head to lord it over him, nor out of his foot to be trodden under him, but out of his side to walk beside him.
   ❏ Like Paul says (1 Cor. 11:11–12), as woman came from man, man now comes from woman and we are all interdependent.

6. Which of the following popular sayings best describes how you feel about relating to other people?
   ❏ "The more people I meet, the more I like my dog."
   ❏ "I love humanity—it's people I can't stand!"
   ❏ "I never met a man (or woman) I didn't like."
   ❏ "People who need people are the luckiest people in the world."
   ❏ "No man (or woman) is an island, apart to himself."
   ❏ other: _____

7. Which type of relationship mentioned in this story do you have the greatest difficulty with?
   ❏ my relationship to God
   ❏ my relationship to animals and the natural world
   ❏ my relationship to the opposite sex
   ❏ my relationship to parents

8. In verse 25 we are told that the man and woman were naked before each other, and in this innocent state they felt no shame. What does this say to you, if you are to have better relationships?
   ❏ I need to stand "spiritually naked" before people.
   ❏ I need to be in a group where others aren't afraid to stand "spiritually naked" before each other.
   ❏ I can't be ashamed of who I am if I am to relate to others.
   ❏ I need to stop being ashamed of my family members.
   ❏ I need to stop being ashamed of my friends.
   ❏ other: _____

CARING TIME / 15–45 Minutes / All Together

Leader: In this first session, take some time to discuss your expectations and to decide on the ground rules for your group. Then spend the remaining time in caring support for each other through sharing and prayer.

1. What motivated you to come to this group?
   ❏ curiosity
   ❏ A friend asked me.
   ❏ I had nothing better to do.
   ❏ a nagging suspicion that I'd better get my life together

EXPECTATIONS

2. As you begin this group, what are some goals or expectations you have for this course? Choose two or three of the following expectations and add one of your own:
   ❏ to understand the components of relationships in my life
   ❏ to strengthen my relationship with God
   ❏ to relax and forget about my relationships for a while
   ❏ to see what the Bible has to say about relationships
   ❏ to take an inventory of the relationships in my life
   ❏ to examine how I relate to family members
   ❏ to discover new ways of relating to people I would normally shun
   ❏ other: _____

3. If you could write your own ground rules for this group, what would you like to insist on? Choose any from the list below, and add one or two of your own:

    ❐ ATTENDANCE: To take the group seriously, and give the meetings priority.

    ❐ QUESTIONS ENCOURAGED: This is a support group for people who are struggling with all sorts of questions, including questions about their spiritual faith. Honest questions are encouraged.

    ❐ MISSION: This group will be "open" to anyone who is struggling, and also to anyone who is seeking or who is starting over in the Christian life ... and it will be the mission of this group to invite new people to the sessions.

    ❐ ACCOUNTABILITY: This group will be a support group. Prayer requests will be shared at the end of every session and group members will be encouraged to call each other to ask, "How's it going?"

    ❐ CONFIDENTIALITY: Anything that is said in the group is kept in confidence.

    ❐ COVENANT: At the end of this course, the group will evaluate the experience and decide if they wish to continue as a covenant group.

SHARING

Take a few minutes to share prayer requests with other group members. Go around and answer this question first:

"How can we help you in prayer this week?"

PRAYER

Take a moment to pray together. If you have not prayed out loud before, finish the sentence:

"Hello, God, this is ... (first name). I want to thank you for ..."

ACTION

1. You now have a brief overview of relationships. Write down two areas of concern you have about a relationship. Refer to these during these sessions, praying that you will discover answers to your concerns.

2. Decide on where the group is going to meet.

3. Ask someone to bring refreshments next week.

4. Encourage the group to invite a friend to the group next week—to fill the "empty chair" (see page 5).

SESSION 2
Loving God

PURPOSE

To discover ways in which our relationship with God is foundational to building all of our relationships.

AGENDA

 **Gathering**   **Bible Study**   **Caring Time**

OPEN

GATHERING / 15 Minutes / All Together

Leader: The purpose of the Gathering time in this session is to help people get to know each other a bit better and share something personal about themselves. We encourage you to be the first one to share with the group. Start with Step One below. Then read Step Two (Introduction) and move on to the Bible Study.

Step One: "God for a Day." If you were elected "God for a Day," which of the following would probably be your first act of office? More serious options are not allowed:

- ❐ throw lightning bolts at people who said I'd "never make it"
- ❐ remove the mosquito (or some other annoying insect) from the face of the earth
- ❐ be right in an argument with my spouse—for once
- ❐ show up in one of Madeline Murray O'Hare's nightmares
- ❐ create real chocolate without fat or cholesterol
- ❐ get my own talk show
- ❐ create an eighth day of the week
- ❐ make an eleventh commandment, namely ...
- ❐ make all vegetables taste like pizza

INTRODUCTION

Step Two: Loving God. Our relationship with God is the most important relationship in our lives. God is the one who created us from the dust of the earth, breathed life into us, redeemed us from our sins and sustains us throughout life. We have often heard the acronym JOY—**J**esus, **O**thers and **Y**ou, for how we are to prioritize our relationships.

What does it mean to love God? We were taught as children to "Love the Lord your God with all your heart and with all your soul and with all your mind. This is the first and greatest commandment." We are to love God unconditionally and totally. We are to love God more than we love anyone else. We are to love God completely. But the question remains—*how* do we love God?

Jesus answered this in a discussion with his disciples: "If you love me you will obey what I command." Or as the apostle John later wrote, "This is the love of God, that we keep his commandments." The answer to that question is also very similar to how we love others. The ways in which we develop a relationship with others is the way we love and develop a relationship with God. We can only know God by spending time with God. J. I. Packer in his book, *Knowing God*, wrote that there is a big difference between "knowing God and knowing about God."

LEADER:
Choose the
OPTION 1 Bible
Study (below)
or the OPTION 2
Study (page 16).

In order to know God, we need to spend time with God studying his Word and praying—talking with God. But prayer also involves listening for God to speak to us as well. We also get to know God through worship and fellowship with other believers. And the key to loving God is obeying his commandments.

In this session, we will be looking at the ways we can know God and develop a relationship with him. In the Option 1 Study (from the Gospel of Mark), we will consider the passage where Jesus states the greatest commandment. In the Option 2 Study (from James' letter), we will look at what James has to say about our relationship with God and how it influences other relationships.

 # BIBLE STUDY / 30 Minutes / Groups of 4

Leader: If you have more than 7 in this session, we recommend groups of 4—but not the same foursomes as last week. Ask one person in each foursome to be the Leader and complete the Bible Study in the time allotted. Remember, you have two choices for Bible Study: Option 1 and Option 2. Then regather for the Caring Time, allowing 15–45 minutes.

OPTION 1

Gospel Study / The Greatest Commandment
Mark 12:28–34

STUDY

Read Mark 12:28–34, and discuss the questions that follow with your group. Religious leaders of Jesus' day spent much time debating the Law, and the question of which of the many commandments in Scripture was the greatest probably came up many times. Here we see Jesus' answer.

28One of the teachers of the law came and heard him debating. Noticing that Jesus had given them a good answer, he asked him, "Of all the commandments, which is the most important?"

29"The most important one," answered Jesus, "is this: 'Hear, O Israel, the Lord our God, the Lord is one. 30Love the Lord your God with all your heart and with all your soul and with all your mind and with all your strength.' 31The second is this: 'Love your neighbor as yourself.' There is no commandment greater than these."

32"Well said, teacher," the man replied. "You are right in saying that God is one and there is no other but him. 33To love him with all your heart, with all your understanding and with all your strength, and to love your neighbor as yourself is more important than all burnt offerings and sacrifices."

34When Jesus saw that he had answered wisely, he said to him, "You are not far from the kingdom of God." And from then on no one dared ask him any more questions.

Mark 12:28–34, NIV

1. From what you see in this passage, how would you describe the relationship between Jesus and this man?
   - ❏ argumentative
   - ❏ respectful
   - ❏ affirming
   - ❏ combative
   - ❏ cautious
   - ❏ mutually probing
   - ❏ competitive
   - ❏ emotionally distant
   - ❏ intellectual
   - ❏ in process

"God created man because God loves and wanted an object to love. He created man so that he could return his love."
—Billy Graham

2. What did Jesus mean when he said to the man, "You are not far from the kingdom of God?"
   - ❏ The kingdom of God was coming soon and he would be a part of it.
   - ❏ The man still had a little growing to do before he could enter the kingdom of God.
   - ❏ He had the right ideas—now he had to develop the right relationship with God.
   - ❏ other: _____

3. Why were people debating the rules and laws with Jesus?
   - ❏ Nobody had written them down.
   - ❏ They were trying out for the debate team.
   - ❏ They liked intellectual exercises.
   - ❏ They were trying to find loopholes so they could do what they wanted.
   - ❏ They were just trying to get the best of Jesus.
   - ❏ These were important things, and they really wanted to know.

4. If these two commandments were all you knew about God's will for the way to live your life, how would it affect your relationships?
   ❑ It wouldn't be sufficient—I wouldn't know what was right and wrong.
   ❑ It would be a good general guide, but I would still have many questions.
   ❑ It would be much simpler than all the confusing rules and laws.
   ❑ I could apply these to all relationships and know how to act.

5. What were the most important "commandments" in your home when you were growing up?
   ❑ "Thou shalt not disturb the sleep of thy parents on Saturday morning!"
   ❑ "Thou shalt wipeth thine feet before entering the house!"
   ❑ "The parents shall not hold him or her guiltless who talketh back!"
   ❑ "Cleaneth thine room or faceth thou the consequences!"
   ❑ "Doeth thine homework before thou watchest the TV!"
   ❑ "Doeth thine own thing, but stayeth out of the way!"
   ❑ other: _____

6. What attitude did you have as an adolescent about "debating" the rules?
   ❑ I didn't have any desire to debate them.
   ❑ I didn't have the courage to debate them.
   ❑ I debated them—but always lost the debate.
   ❑ I debated them often—and occasionally won.
   ❑ I debated them constantly—and generally won.
   ❑ I debated them often, but wish I would have lost.
   ❑ other: _____

7. How are you doing right now at loving God in the ways we are commanded to?

   WITH ALL YOUR HEART: making the relationship heartfelt, instead of merely intellectual

1	2	3	4	5	6	7	8	9	10
I'm a wipeout.				I'm struggling.					I'm on target.

   WITH ALL YOUR SOUL: with total spiritual devotion, disciplining yourself through prayer and meditation

1	2	3	4	5	6	7	8	9	10
I'm a wipeout.				I'm struggling.					I'm on target.

"Before we were born, God was God, the Lord God Almighty! He has never needed us. None of our human talents and abilities are significant to him. But he needs our love and wants our love."
—A. W. Tozer

15

LEADER: When you have completed the Bible Study, move on to the Caring Time (page 19).

WITH ALL YOUR MIND: by learning all you can about God's will

1	2	3	4	5	6	7	8	9	10
I'm a wipeout.				I'm struggling.					I'm on target.

WITH ALL YOUR STRENGTH: by giving your time and energy to God's work

1	2	3	4	5	6	7	8	9	10
I'm a wipeout.				I'm struggling.					I'm on target.

8. What do you need to do to love God more fully?
   ❒ learn more about God through going to church and Bible study
   ❒ let God touch my heart more fully
   ❒ give more of my time and energy to God's work
   ❒ love God through loving my neighbors, who are his children
   ❒ other: _____

OPTION 2

Epistle Study / Resisting Satan
James 4:1–10

STUDY

Read James 4:1–10 and share your responses to the following questions with your group.

4 *What causes fights and quarrels among you? Don't they come from your desires that battle within you? ²You want something but don't get it. You kill and covet, but you cannot have what you want. You quarrel and fight. You do not have, because you do not ask God. ³When you ask, you do not receive, because you ask with wrong motives, that you may spend what you get on your pleasures.*

⁴You adulterous people, don't you know that friendship with the world is hatred toward God? Anyone who chooses to be a friend of the world becomes an enemy of God. ⁵Or do you think Scripture says without reason that the spirit he caused to live in us envies intensely? ⁶But he gives us more grace. That is why Scripture says:

> *"God opposes the proud*
> *but gives grace to the humble."*

⁷Submit yourselves, then, to God. Resist the devil, and he will flee from you. ⁸Come near to God and he will come near to you. Wash your hands, you sinners, and purify your hearts, you double-minded. ⁹Grieve, mourn and wail. Change your laughter to mourning and your joy to gloom.
¹⁰Humble yourselves before the Lord, and he will lift you up.

James 4:1–10, NIV

1. What is your initial reaction to this passage?
   ❏ Sounds like my parents when they lectured me and my siblings.
   ❏ Sounds like James was being kind of judgmental himself.
   ❏ Sounds like it could have been written about people in our day.
   ❏ This is no-nonsense "telling it like it is" in moral matters.

2. What does James mean when he says, "friendship with the world is hatred toward God"?
   ❏ God and the world aren't on speaking terms.
   ❏ You cannot value what God values and also value what the world values.
   ❏ If you listen to what the world says, you will end up hating God.
   ❏ other: _____

3. What is your reaction to James' teaching, "Come near to God and he will come near to you"?
   ❏ It couldn't be that simple.
   ❏ I've tried to come near to God, but I can't find him.
   ❏ I'm not sure I want to come near to God.
   ❏ It's been true in my life—every time I move toward him, God responds.

4. Who were you most likely to have "fights and quarrels" with when you were in the fifth grade?
   ❏ my brother   ❏ my father
   ❏ my sister   ❏ my mother
   ❏ another kid in school   ❏ other: _____
   ❏ another kid in the neighborhood

5. What did you usually fight about with the person in question #4?
   ❏ over the attention of another friend
   ❏ over playing with my stuff
   ❏ over chores around the house
   ❏ over who was right and who was wrong in an argument
   ❏ other: _____

6. What desires do you have that sometimes lead to quarrels with other people?
   ❏ my desire for control
   ❏ my desire for what other people have
   ❏ my desire to be right
   ❏ my desire to avoid change
   ❏ other: _____

7. What kind of quarrels with God are you most likely to have?
   ❒ like Tevye in *Fiddler on the Roof*—over why I'm not a rich man (woman)
   ❒ over why there's so much pain and suffering in the world
   ❒ over what God wants to do in my life
   ❒ over why my prayers never seem to get answered
   ❒ other: _____

8. Using the scale below, rank yourself on the following things James instructs us to do in our relationship with God:

1	2	3	4	5	6	7	8	9	10
I never even think of doing this.			This is part of my spiritual life.				This is an integral part of my spiritual life.		

   ___SUBMIT TO GOD: as opposed to following the ways of the world

   ___HUMILITY: to see your need for God's grace

   ___RESIST THE DEVIL: Submission to God begins with resisting Satan's enticements, rather than giving in to them.

   ___PRAY AND ASK GOD: We should not ask with the wrong motives.

   ___ FRIENDSHIP WITH GOD: We cannot be friends with the world and with God.

   ___WASH YOUR HANDS: a symbol for the inner purity God desires

   ___PURIFY YOUR HEARTS: Cleanse yourself from all the ways of the world.

   ___GRIEVE, MOURN, WAIL: With a sense of finality, leave your former life behind; a strong reaction to sin.

   ___SINGLE-MINDED: We are to be single-minded in our loyalty to Christ.

LEADER: When you have completed the Bible Study, move on to the Caring Time (page 19).

9. Which action helps you to follow James' instruction and "come near to God"?
   ❒ regular family (or private) devotions
   ❒ times of prayer and meditation
   ❒ church attendance
   ❒ getting out into nature
   ❒ being part of a loving Christian fellowship
   ❒ other: _____

CARING TIME / 15–45 Minutes / All Together

Leader: The purpose of the Caring Time in this session is to spend time in caring support for each other through Sharing, Prayer and Action.

SHARING

Get together with one other person in the group and share:

> *"In what area of your life do you need to strengthen your relationship with God?"*

PRAYER

Gather your group in a circle and pray for the concerns and struggles that were voiced during this meeting. If you would like to pray in silence, say the word "Amen" when you finish, so that the next person will know when to start.

ACTION

Plan three concrete steps you can take this week to strengthen your relationship to God in the area you mentioned in the sharing time above. List these steps in a prayer to God asking for his help, promising him your diligence, and listening for his direction.

SESSION 3
Loving Ourselves

PURPOSE

To discover ways to love ourselves.

AGENDA

 **Gathering**   **Bible Study**   **Caring Time**

OPEN

 ## GATHERING / 15 Minutes / All Together

Leader: Read the instructions for Step One and set the pace by going first. Then read the Introduction in Step Two and move on to the Bible Study.

Step One: Self-Affirmation. We all need a pat on the back from time to time. Sometimes we need to pat ourselves on the back—not in a boastful or arrogant way, but as a means of affirming who we are. Choose two of the following and share your responses with the group:

- ❏ Two things I like about my appearance are ...
- ❏ Two things I do to keep myself healthy are ...
- ❏ Two jobs I do very well at work are ...
- ❏ One thing I do to maintain a good friendship is ...
- ❏ One positive thing others have said about me is ...

INTRODUCTION

Step Two: Loving Ourselves. There have been numerous books written on love over the centuries. In fact, it may be the most popular subject ever written about. Leo Buscaglia, in his book *Love*, writes that in discussing love one needs to consider the following:

- One cannot give what he does not possess. To give love you must possess love.
- One cannot teach what he does not understand. To teach love you must comprehend love.
- One cannot know what he does not study. To study love you must live in love.
- One cannot appreciate what he does not recognize. To recognize love you must be receptive to love.
- One cannot have doubt about that which he wishes to trust. To trust love you must be convinced of love.

- One cannot admit what he does not yield to. To yield to love you must be vulnerable to love.
- One cannot live what he does not dedicate himself to. To dedicate yourself to love you must be forever growing in love.

We are not talking about some sort of ego trip. We are talking about somebody who really cares about himself. As Buscaglia writes, "Everything is filtered through me, and so the greater I am, the more I have to give. The greater knowledge that I have, the more I'm going to have to give. The greater understanding I have, the greater is my ability to teach others and to make myself the most fantastic, the most beautiful, the most wondrous, the most tender human being in the world."

Loving oneself does not imply ego-centered reality like the old witch in *Snow White*. She reveled in the process of gazing into her mirror and asking, "Mirror, mirror on the wall, who is the fairest one of all?" Loving oneself does mean a genuine caring, concern, and respect for oneself. To care about oneself is basic to love. Humans love themselves when they clearly see themselves and genuinely appreciate what they see. But they are especially excited and challenged with the prospect of what they can become. To love ourselves we must discover and celebrate our uniqueness. And this includes living up to our potential. Herbert Otto says only about five percent of our human potential is realized in our lifetime. What about the other 95 percent?

Loving yourself also involves the knowledge that only you can be you. If you try to be like anyone else, you may come very close, but you will always be second best. But, *you* are the best you. It is the easiest, most practical, most rewarding thing to be. Then it makes sense that you can only be to others what you are to yourself. Buscaglia writes, "If you know, accept and appreciate yourself and your uniqueness, you will permit others to do so. If you value and appreciate the discovery of yourself, you will encourage others to engage in self-discovery. If you recognize your need to be free to discover who you are, you will allow others their freedom to do so, also. When you realize you are the best you, you will accept the fact that others are the best they. But it follows that it all starts with you. To the extent to which you know yourself, and we are all more alike than different, you can know others. When you love yourself, you will love others. And to the depth and extent to which you can love yourself, only to that extent and depth will you be able to love others."

LEADER: Choose the OPTION 1 Bible Study (page 22) or the OPTION 2 Study (page 25).

In Option 1, we will study the story of Peter's denial and his need to accept himself for who he really was. In accepting his failures, he could love himself as Christ loved him. And in Option 2, we will study a passage from John's first epistle, where he explains the relationship between loving God and loving ourselves.

BIBLE STUDY / 30 Minutes / Groups of 4

Leader: Help the group decide on Option 1 or Option 2 for their Bible Study. If there are 7 or more in the group, encourage them to move into groups of 4. Ask one person in each group to be the Leader. The Leader guides the sharing and makes sure that each group member has an opportunity to answer every question.

OPTION 1

Gospel Study / Realizing Our Potential
Mark 14:27–31,66–72

STUDY

Peter protests that he will not betray Jesus, but events show that he (as well as others) does this very thing. In the context of the disciple's commitment to Jesus, this marks the lowest point. This experience reveals to them the tentativeness and self-interest that characterized their faith thus far. Read Mark 14:27–31, 66–72 and discuss your responses to the following questions with the group.

> 27"You will all fall away," Jesus told them, "for it is written:
>
> " 'I will strike the shepherd,
>   and the sheep will be scattered.'

28But after I have risen, I will go ahead of you into Galilee."

29Peter declared, "Even if all fall away, I will not."

30"I tell you the truth," Jesus answered, "today—yes, even tonight—before the rooster crows twice you yourself will disown me three times."

31But Peter insisted emphatically, "Even if I have to die with you, I will never disown you." And all the others said the same. ...

66While Peter was below in the courtyard, one of the servant girls of the high priest came by. 67When she saw Peter warming himself, she looked closely at him.

"You also were with that Nazarene, Jesus," she said.

68But he denied it. "I don't know or understand what you're talking about," he replied, and went out into the entryway.

69When the servant girl saw him there, she said again to those standing around, "This fellow is one of them." 70Again he denied it.

After a little while, those standing near said to Peter, "Surely you are one of them, for you are a Galilean."

71He began to call down curses on himself, and he swore to them, "I don't know this man you're talking about."

72Immediately the rooster crowed the second time. Then Peter remembered the word Jesus had spoken to him: "Before the rooster crows twice you will disown me three times." And he broke down and wept.

Mark 14:27–31,66–72, NIV

22

1. Imagine that you were a reporter for *The Jerusalem Journal*, and you were assigned to interview Peter after these events. What would be the first question you would ask him?
   ❏ "So, Peter, how does it feel to be a turncoat?"
   ❏ "Didn't you even think about Jesus' prediction?"
   ❏ "Do you think Jesus could have stopped you from making this mistake?"
   ❏ "How has this changed the way you look at yourself?"
   ❏ "What do you plan to do now to make up for this?"
   ❏ other: _____

2. What is your reaction to Peter's denial of Jesus?
   ❏ I probably would have done the same thing.
   ❏ He was a coward.
   ❏ I pity him.
   ❏ I can't believe he would do something that dumb.
   ❏ I'm angry at him.
   ❏ other: _____

3. If you could put in a good word for Peter, what would it be?
   ❏ He meant well.   ❏ He couldn't help it.
   ❏ He came back.   ❏ He's only human.
   ❏ He didn't know himself.   ❏ He was confused.
   ❏ He probably had a rough childhood.

4. After his denial, why do you think Jesus chose Peter and changed his name from Simon ("sinking sand") to Peter ("the rock")?
   ❏ Peter was the best man available.
   ❏ Jesus believed in positive thinking.
   ❏ Jesus believed that despite his flaws, Peter would do fine.
   ❏ Jesus wanted to illustrate the power of God.
   ❏ Jesus knew Peter's potential better than Peter did himself.

5. What impact do you think this failure had on Peter's future?
   ❏ It probably made him less cocky.
   ❏ It probably made him less self-confident.
   ❏ It probably made him a more sensitive person.
   ❏ It probably made him into the man of God he became.

6. Who do you remember failing when you were in high school?
   ❏ my parents   ❏ one of my teachers
   ❏ my best friend   ❏ one of my employees
   ❏ a relative   ❏ myself
   ❏ a brother or sister   ❏ nobody
   ❏ my youth leader   ❏ other: _____

7. What helped you recover your self image after this failure?
   ❒ the person's forgiveness
   ❒ praying to God
   ❒ making up for it by doing something good
   ❒ just forgetting about it and putting it behind me
   ❒ I never did recover it.

8. How do you usually react to failure?
   ❒ I run away from the situation.   ❒ I kick myself for days.
   ❒ I hide my feelings from everyone.   ❒ I spend time with God.
   ❒ I ask for forgiveness and move on.   ❒ I forget about it.
   ❒ I do penance.   ❒ other: _____

9. How do you usually feel about yourself with respect to each of the areas listed below? Mark an "**X**" on the following scale:

   MY PHYSICAL SELF:
   I feel great._____I don't like myself.

   MY SOCIAL SELF:
   I feel great._____I don't like myself.

   MY EMOTIONAL SELF:
   I feel great._____I don't like myself.

   MY INTELLECTUAL SELF:
   I feel great._____I don't like myself.

   MY SPIRITUAL SELF:
   I feel great._____I don't like myself.

10. What would you need to do to show the same grace toward yourself that Jesus showed to Peter?
    ❒ cut myself a break
    ❒ treat myself to something special
    ❒ forgive myself
    ❒ show myself some kindness
    ❒ nothing—I feel great about myself
    ❒ other: _____

LEADER: When you have completed the Bible Study, move on to the Caring Time (page 28).

When Jesus chose Peter as his disciple and friend, he knew who Peter was. Jesus saw Peter's rough edges, but he also saw Peter's heart. Jesus knew that Peter had potential. From the very beginning, Jesus encouraged Peter and thought the best of him: "You will be called Cephas, and on this rock I will build my church." Evidently Jesus saw something Peter couldn't see in himself.

Peter and Jesus' lives overlapped quite a bit during their friendship. Through many of their encounters, Peter experienced a roller-coaster ride of emotions. Peter felt honored (and scared) to be called by Jesus. He was thrilled when Jesus healed his mother-in-law. Peter tried to rebuke Jesus when Jesus said that he (Jesus) was going to have to suffer and die. Peter went from a spiritual high (at the Transfiguration) to a spiritual low (at Gethsemane). Peter must have been heartsick when he heard the rooster crow after his threefold denial of Jesus; his confident assertion that he would never deny Jesus meant nothing in light of his actions. But Jesus knew that that wasn't the end of the story. To assure Peter of his unconditional love, Jesus affirmed Peter three times following the resurrection—one time for each of Peter's denials.

OPTION 2

Epistle Study / Children of God
1 John 2:28–3:3

STUDY

The apostle John emphasized loving others above all other teaching, and showed how loving God was integrally related to loving others. However, in the following passage, he also writes about how God's love for us gives us a status that helps us to love ourselves. Read 1 John 2:28–3:3, and discuss the questions which follow with your group.

28And now dear children, continue in him, so that when he appears we may be confident and unashamed before him at his coming.
29If you know that he is righteous, you know that everyone who does what is right has been born of him.
3 How great is the love the Father has lavished on us, that we should be called children of God! And that is what we are! The reason the world does not know us is that it did not know him. 2Dear friends, now we are children of God, and what we will be has not yet been made known. But we know that when he appears, we shall be like him, for we shall see him as he is. 3Everyone who has this hope in him purifies himself, just as he is pure.
1 John 2:28–3:3, NIV

25

1. What is your first impression of the teaching of this passage?
   ❏ If I'm a child of God, I must be the black sheep of the family.
   ❏ If we are all children of God, how come we don't act more like family?
   ❏ I believe I'm God's child, but sometimes I wonder why God doesn't disown me.
   ❏ My status as God's child is at the heart of my self-worth.
   ❏ other: _____

2. What is necessary for a person to be "confident and unashamed" at Christ's coming?
   ❏ You have to have taken the Dale Carnegie course.
   ❏ You have to be a positive thinker.
   ❏ You have to live right.
   ❏ You have to believe in Christ and follow him as Lord.

"If the believer yields to the flesh, he is enslaved by it, but if he obeys the prompting of the Spirit, he is liberated."
—F. F. Bruce

3. What does it mean to you that when Christ appears we shall be like him (3:2)?
   ❏ We'll all wear robes and have beards.
   ❏ We'll all have his special power.
   ❏ We'll have conformed ourselves to God's will, as Christ has.
   ❏ We'll have his spiritual nature.

4. John says, "what we will be has not yet been made known." When you were a child, what did you want to be when you grew up?

5. As you think of "what you will be" now, how do you want your life to be different five years from now?

6. What does it mean to you that right now you are a child of God?
   ❏ I don't have to wait for a future accomplishment to have worth.
   ❏ I don't have to rely on a human relationship to have worth.
   ❏ I have a worth before God that will not be taken away from me.
   ❏ I have a relationship of kinship with all of humanity.
   ❏ other: _____

7. On the scales below, mark to what degree you feel "uncertain and ashamed" or "confident and unashamed" in each of these areas:

IN MY FAITHFULNESS IN MY PRAYER AND DEVOTIONAL LIFE:

1	2	3	4	5	6	7	8	9	10

uncertain and ashamed   confident and unashamed

IN THE WAY I TREAT MY BROTHERS AND SISTERS:

1	2	3	4	5	6	7	8	9	10

uncertain and ashamed   confident and unashamed

IN THE FAITH I HAVE IN JESUS CHRIST:

1	2	3	4	5	6	7	8	9	10

uncertain and ashamed   confident and unashamed

LEADER: When you have completed the Bible Study, move on to the Caring Time (page 28).

8. What would it mean for you to "purify yourself, just as Christ is pure"?
   ❏ removing the bitterness in my life by forgiving someone else
   ❏ removing the guilt and shame in my life by accepting God's forgiveness
   ❏ removing the uncertainty in my life by trusting God's promises
   ❏ I don't think I can be purified in such a way.
   ❏ I don't think I want to be purified in such a way.

CARING TIME / 15–45 Minutes / All Together

Leader: Bring all of the foursomes back together for a time of caring through Sharing, Prayer and Action.

SHARING

Honey for My Ears. Has someone ever told you something that made you feel great? What would you like to hear every now and then that would make you feel special? Choose one of the general statements listed below, and tell your group what you would like to hear. Enjoy it as group members take turns telling you what you would like to hear.

I really enjoy it when someone says ...

❏ something that recognizes my abilities.

❏ that they've noticed my personal growth.

❏ that I've inspired them in some way.

❏ something positive about the way I look.

❏ that there is something about me that they want to emulate.

❏ that they care how I feel.

❏ something that tells me I'm loved unconditionally.

❏ something that tells me I'm forgiven.

❏ that there is something about me that reminds them of Jesus.

PRAYER

Conclude your meeting with a time of sharing concerns and prayer requests. During your time of prayer, remember the person next to you and what they shared with you. You may say your prayer in silence, ending with a verbal "Amen," so that the next person will know when to start.

ACTION

1. Remember your neighbor's prayer request throughout the week. Drop him/her a note of encouragement with respect to their prayer request.

2. Reflect on the following Scripture passage from this study throughout the week:

   Dear friends, now we are children of God, and what we will be has not yet been made known. But we do know that when he appears, we shall be like him, for we shall see him as he is.

   1 John 3:2

SESSION 4
Loving Family

PURPOSE | To learn how to deal with "difficult" family members.

AGENDA |  Gathering Bible Study Caring Time

OPEN

 GATHERING / 15 Minutes / All Together
Leader: Read the instructions for Step One and set the pace by going first. Then read the Introduction in Step Two and move on to the Bible Study.

Step One: My Family. What was your family like? Or what is your family like? Help your group understand your family. Select a comic strip which best describes your family. Tell the group what you have chosen and feel free to briefly explain your selection. If my family was a comic strip, it would be:

❑ *Blondie*   ❑ *Dennis the Menace*
❑ *Family Circus*   ❑ *The Far Side*
❑ *Hagar the Horrible*   ❑ *Andy Capp*
❑ *Calvin and Hobbes*   ❑ *For Better, For Worse*
❑ *Peanuts*   ❑ *Cathy*
❑ *B.C.*   ❑ *other:* _____

INTRODUCTION | **Step Two: Loving Family.** Let's admit it—at times the most difficult people to love are family members. On the surface we say that we love them, because that is what is expected of us. There are simply some people whose personalities "rub us the wrong way." If we met those persons at a company picnic or at the grocery store, we could avoid them. However, if we meet them at a family dinner, there is little that we can do. "You can pick your friends, but you can't pick your family." Deep down, some family members may be extremely difficult to love. Perhaps they have disappointed us or hurt us. Because of the closeness of the relationships, we usually feel the pain more deeply when we are hurt by a family member.

Even the most loving families experience friction when people live under the same roof. Some of this conflict is usually just light banter and produces little hostility or pain. The strains of keeping a marriage healthy, raising children and making ends meet combine to make fertile soil for family conflict. Who's going to feed the baby at 3 a.m.? Who tracked mud all over the clean kitchen floor? Who splurged on a new gadget and wiped out the monthly budget?

While family conflict is inevitable, it does not have to blow a family apart. Through loving patience and understanding, conflict can actually strengthen a loving family relationship. Communication is the key. Solutions to conflict can usually be found when members are able to freely talk and listen without being devastated. Sometimes, however, outside help is needed, and a family should feel free to call on a minister or a professional counselor when necessary.

Parenting adolescents can be the most strain-filled family relationship. Adolescents experience bodily changes (including those wild hormones) and struggle with their identity. The adolescent tests boundaries and tries out new behaviors in search of that identity. The challenge of parenting at this time is keeping firm boundaries in line, while at the same time encouraging independence and self-exploration. Conflict is a common experience in families with children of this age.

LEADER: Choose the OPTION 1 Bible Study (below) or the OPTION 2 Study (page 34).

In the following Option 1 Study (from Luke's Gospel), we will see a father's pain and a son's rebellion turn into a tearful reunion. And in Option 2 (from Paul's letter to the Ephesians), we will see how Paul addresses the relationships of husbands and wives, and parents and children. Remember, the purpose of the Bible Study is to talk about your family relationships.

BIBLE STUDY / 30 Minutes / Groups of 4

Leader: Help the groups decide on the Option 1 or Option 2 Bible Study. If there are more than 7 people, divide into groups of 4, and ask one person in each group to be the Leader. Finish the Bible Study in 30 minutes, and gather the groups together for the Caring Time.

Gospel Study / A Family Conflict
Luke 15:11–32

Read Luke 15:11–32 and discuss your responses to the following questions with your group. This is one of Jesus' most famous parables, and was told in response to the outrage of the Pharisees (the religious leaders of the time) over Jesus' association with people who were "sinners."

11Jesus continued: "There was a man who had two sons. 12The younger one said to his father, 'Father, give me my share of the estate.' So he divided his property between them.

13"Not long after that, the younger son got together all he had, set off for a distant country and there squandered his wealth in wild living. 14After he had spent everything, there was a severe famine in that whole country, and he began to be in need. 15So he went and hired himself out to a citizen of that country, who sent him to his fields to feed pigs. 16He longed to fill his stomach with the pods that the pigs were eating, but no one gave him anything.

17"When he came to his senses, he said, 'How many of my father's hired men have food to spare, and here I am starving to death! 18I will set out and go back to my father and say to him: Father, I have sinned against heaven and against you. 19I am no longer worthy to be called your son; make me like one of your hired men.' 20So he got up and went to his father.

"But while he was still a long way off, his father saw him and was filled with compassion for him; he ran to his son, threw his arms around him and kissed him.

21"The son said to him, 'Father, I have sinned against heaven and against you. I am no longer worthy to be called your son.'

22"But the father said to his servants, 'Quick! Bring the best robe and put it on him. Put a ring on his finger and sandals on his feet. 23Bring the fattened calf and kill it. Let's have a feast and celebrate. 24For this son of mine was dead and is alive again; he was lost and is found.' So they began to celebrate.

25"Meanwhile, the older son was in the field. When he came near the house, he heard music and dancing. 26So he called one of the servants and asked him what was going on. 27'Your brother has come,' he replied, 'and your father has killed the fattened calf because he has him back safe and sound.'

28"The older brother became angry and refused to go in. So his father went out and pleaded with him. 29But he answered his father, 'Look! All these years I've been slaving for you and never disobeyed your orders. Yet you never gave me even a young goat so I could celebrate with my friends. 30But when this son of yours who has squandered your property with prostitutes comes home, you kill the fattened calf for him!'

31" 'My son,' the father said, 'you are always with me, and everything I have is yours. 32But we had to celebrate and be glad, because this brother of yours was dead and is alive again; he was lost and is found.' "

Luke 15:11–32, NIV

1. Which character do you identify with in this story? Why?
   - ❐ the younger son—I've squandered my allowance (and even sown a few wild oats).
   - ❐ the older son—I've resented younger siblings who got privileges I didn't.
   - ❐ the waiting father—My kids keep me up at night.
   - ❐ the narrator—I'm a spectator watching what God is doing.
   - ❐ the younger son—I've experienced grace despite my actions.
   - ❐ the older son—I've felt that I've had to be good.
   - ❐ the pigs—I've been with prodigals who have hit bottom.

2. Why did the younger son leave home in the first place?
   - ❐ He wanted to party.
   - ❐ He was tired of being told what to do.
   - ❐ He thought that he was more mature than he was.
   - ❐ He wasn't considerate of the needs of his family.
   - ❐ He had to try his own wings and make his own mistakes.
   - ❐ He wasn't into delayed gratification.
   - ❐ He had to get out from under the shadow of his older brother.
   - ❐ He had a big fight with his dad.

3. Why did the older brother stay home?
   - ❐ He was too chicken to do anything else.
   - ❐ He loved his father.
   - ❐ He was a mama's boy.
   - ❐ He was smarter financially—he wanted to build the business.
   - ❐ He believed that obedience would be rewarded.
   - ❐ Now that his younger brother was gone, he didn't have any competition for his father's attention.
   - ❐ He was a workaholic.

4. Why did the father let the younger son leave so easily?
   - ❐ He had no control over his younger son.
   - ❐ His son would leave no matter what he did.
   - ❐ He knew his son would have to learn about life the hard way.
   - ❐ He didn't care what his younger son did.
   - ❐ He was glad to get rid of the troublemaker.
   - ❐ He was relieved that the younger son finally left.

5. When did you leave home for the first time? What were some of the circumstances surrounding your departure? Where did you go when you left your parents' home? What were some of your feelings at that time?

6. When the younger son returned home, what would have been your response (as his parent)?
   - ❑ Good to see you—but you're grounded.
   - ❑ You have disgraced this family.
   - ❑ Where's the money?
   - ❑ I don't approve of your actions, but you're still my son.
   - ❑ Welcome home, son—I love you.
   - ❑ Do you realize how much your mother and I have worried about you all this time?

7. If you were the older son, what would you do next?
   - ❑ go off on my own partying binge
   - ❑ go in and join my younger brother's party
   - ❑ stay outside and sulk for the rest of my life
   - ❑ go in and ruin the party for everyone else
   - ❑ go back to work and try not to think about it
   - ❑ go in and make my younger brother feel really guilty

8. Who has played the "older brother" in your life—the one who was always jealous whenever anything good happened to you?
   - ❑ an older brother/sister
   - ❑ a younger brother/sister
   - ❑ a parent
   - ❑ a co-worker
   - ❑ an ex-spouse
   - ❑ a friend
   - ❑ no one
   - ❑ other: _____

9. One way we can strengthen our family relationships is by resolving conflicts. Which of the patterns for resolving family conflict in this story are typical of you and/or family members?
   - ❑ insist on doing things my way, right or wrong
   - ❑ tow the line; give in to "father knows best"
   - ❑ lovingly let people suffer the consequences of their own decisions
   - ❑ stick to my own business, avoid the conflict and let time heal all wounds
   - ❑ vent my disappointment and anger
   - ❑ avoid the conflict at all costs

LEADER: When you have completed the Bible Study, move on to the Caring Time (page 37).

10. Which relationship in your family generates the most conflict? Why?
    - ❑ father and son
    - ❑ mother and son
    - ❑ brother and brother
    - ❑ sister and brother
    - ❑ myself and an in-law
    - ❑ father and daughter
    - ❑ mother and daughter
    - ❑ sister and sister
    - ❑ husband and wife
    - ❑ other: _____

11. What healing change would need to happen in your family for you to want to party and celebrate in the way this father celebrated with his son?

Under Jewish law, the younger of two sons would receive one-third of the estate upon his father's death (Deut. 21:17). Even though a father could divide up his property before he died, this son's request would be considered unbelievably callous. It implies that the fact that his father is alive interferes with his plans. The father willingly divides his property between his sons. The expectation is that while the land legally belongs to the sons, they are morally obliged to provide for their father while he is alive.

The son sold off his share of the estate, so that he could have cash to do what he wanted! This act was scandalous, since a person's identity and future was tied to his family's land. By selling it off, he separated himself from his family, lost his means of income, and robbed future descendants of the security of owning land.

OPTION 2

Epistle Study / Family Relations
Ephesians 5:21–6:4

STUDY

Read Ephesians 5:21–6:4, and discuss the questions which follow with your group. In this passage, Paul encourages Christians to treat each other lovingly in relationships.

[21]Submit to one another out of reverence for Christ.

[22]Wives, submit to your husbands as to the Lord. [23]For the husband is the head of the wife as Christ is the head of the church, his body, of which he is the Savior. [24]Now as the church submits to Christ, so also wives should submit to their husbands in everything.

[25]Husbands, love your wives, just as Christ loved the church and gave himself up for her [26]to make her holy, cleansing her by the washing with water through the word, [27]and to present her to himself as a radiant church, without stain or wrinkle or any other blemish, but holy and blameless. [28]In this same way, husbands ought to love their wives as their own bodies. He who loves his wife loves himself. [29]After all, no one ever hated his own body, but he feeds and cares for it, just as Christ does the church— [30]for we are members of his body. [31]"For this reason a man will leave his father and mother and be united to his wife, and the two will become one flesh." [32]This is a profound mystery—but I am talking about Christ and the church. [33]However, each one of you also must love his wife as he loves himself, and the wife must respect her husband.

6 *Children, obey your parents in the Lord, for this is right. [2]"Honor your father and mother"—which is the first commandment with a promise— [3]"that it may go well with you and that you may enjoy long life on the earth."*

[4]Fathers, do not exasperate your children; instead, bring them up in the training and instruction of the Lord.

Ephesians 5:21–6:4, NIV

1. Which of the following TV families best exemplifies this passage?
   - ❒ the Taylors *(Home Improvement)*
   - ❒ the Cleavers *(Leave It to Beaver)*
   - ❒ the Andersons *(Father Knows Best)*
   - ❒ the Connors *(Roseanne)*
   - ❒ the Huxtables *(The Cosby Show)*
   - ❒ the Simpsons
   - ❒ other: _____

2. What part of this passage is the most difficult for you to understand?
   - ❒ that husbands are supposed to emulate Christ in their love for their wives
   - ❒ that Paul calls *all* of us to submit to each other (v. 21)
   - ❒ that Paul connects a Scripture about marriage to Christ and the church
   - ❒ that obeying my parents has an effect on my future
   - ❒ I don't have a hard time with any of it.
   - ❒ other: _____

3. How are husbands to love their wives "just as Christ loved the church and gave himself up for her"?
   - ❒ A husband needs to "give himself up" (relinquish his own desires) for his wife.
   - ❒ A husband needs to be willing to die for his wife and family.
   - ❒ A husband is to love his wife no matter what.
   - ❒ A husband's love needs to be selfless.
   - ❒ other: _____

4. Wives are called to "submit" and husbands are called to "love." Can you love without submitting to the other person? Why or why not?

5. Having read this passage, what would you now say is the responsibility of husband and wife to submit in the marriage relationship?
   - ❒ The wife should always submit to the will of her husband.
   - ❒ The wife should submit to the will of her husband most of the time.
   - ❒ Both husband and wife should submit to each other equally.
   - ❒ Both the husband and wife should submit to the greater good of the marriage.
   - ❒ "Submission" is a dirty word—I say, "fight it out to the end!"

6. In your parents' marriage, what was the role of submission?
   - ❏ It was always my mother's role—she was a doormat.
   - ❏ It was always my father's role—he was "henpecked."
   - ❏ It was something neither one ever did—they fought every step of the way.
   - ❏ It was something either parent could do when the occasion called for it.
   - ❏ Not applicable—I lived with only one parent.
   - ❏ other: _____

7. In what area of your marital life do both partners resist submitting to the needs or perspectives of the other?
   - ❏ in who holds the VCR remote
   - ❏ in who drives the nicer car
   - ❏ in making major purchases
   - ❏ in trying to balance our professions
   - ❏ in dealing with our children
   - ❏ in sexual matters
   - ❏ in all we do
   - ❏ This never happens with us.

"A family is where principles are hammered and honed on the anvil of everyday living."
—Charles Swindoll

8. Husbands are directed by Paul to "love your wives." What shared experiences have strengthened that love and made it an easier command to follow? (For singles: What shared experiences do you think would strengthen love?)
   - ❏ our early romantic experiences
   - ❏ going through hard times together
   - ❏ her support of my career
   - ❏ having a child together
   - ❏ her faith in God
   - ❏ other: _____

9. Wives are told by Paul to "respect your husbands." What has your husband done to increase the respect you feel for him? (For singles: What would increase the respect of a wife for her husband?)
   - ❏ his accomplishments in his career
   - ❏ his support of my career
   - ❏ his devotion to our family
   - ❏ his desire for equality in our marriage
   - ❏ his faith in God
   - ❏ other: _____

LEADER: When you have completed the Bible Study, move on to the Caring Time (page 37).

10. If you were to love the people in your present family situation "as Christ loves the church," how would it change your family?

CARING TIME / 15–45 Minutes / All Together

Leader: The purpose of the Caring Time in this session is to spend time in caring support for each other through Sharing, Prayer and Action.

SHARING

Share your response to the following question with your group:

"How can I strengthen my relationship with my family?"

PRAYER

Gather your group in a circle and pray for the concerns and struggles voiced during this meeting. If you want to pray in silence, say the word "Amen" when you finish your prayer, so that the next person will know when to start.

ACTION

Plan two or three concrete steps you can take this week to demonstrate your love for your family.

SESSION 5
Loving Others: Inside the Community of Faith

PURPOSE | To discover what it means to love others within the community of faith.

AGENDA |  **Gathering** **Bible Study** **Caring Time**

OPEN

GATHERING / 15 Minutes / All Together

Leader: Read the Instructions for Step One and go first. Then read the Introduction (Step 2) and explain the two Bible Study choices.

Step One: Relationships. How are you doing in your relationships? Choose a "circle" of relationships, such as family, coworkers, friends, your group members, etc. From the choices below, select the answer which best describes your recent behavior among the relationships you have chosen. Tell the group how you see yourself in those relationships, and how the other people might have seen you.

❒ SAINT SWEETHEART: I couldn't be nicer.

❒ MICKEY MOUSE: I listen so much, I'm all ears!

❒ A DOORMAT: People have been wiping their feet on me.

❒ TEDDY BEAR: I seem to comfort people.

❒ A GRIZZLY BEAR: Watch out! I may bite!

❒ MOTHER HEN: Cluck! Cluck! Who needs me now?

❒ SELFISH SHELLFISH: Keep your hands off my pearl!

❒ THE GRINCH: I seem to ruin everyone's fun.

❒ ST. NICK: All I do is give, give, give.

❒ ALADDIN'S GENIE: I can grant wishes!

❒ BENEDICT ARNOLD: I feel like a traitor.

❒ DRACULA: People are afraid of me.

Step Two: Loving Others: Inside the Community of Faith. Being a member of the Christian family is similar to membership in any family. There is a strong common bond which unites us. But that doesn't mean that we will always agree with other family members (or that we will always get along). What is our responsibility to fellow believers? Two of our major responsibilities are having an attitude of servanthood and working toward unity.

"There is no higher religion than human service. To work for the common good is the greatest creed."
—Albert Schweitzer

In the 1980s, we were concerned with self-fulfillment. In the '90s, we are moving away from the self-fulfillment perspective to a desire to give ourselves to something beyond ourselves—to serve others. Albert Schweitzer said repeatedly that as long as there was a person in the world who was hungry, sick, lonely or living in fear, that person was his responsibility. He affirmed this by living a life based on this belief—a life of servanthood. The love of humanity is a natural outgrowth of love for a single individual. Herbert Otto states: "Only in a continuing relationship is there a possibility for love to become deeper and fuller so that it envelops all our life and extends into the community." We grow as we help others. As we meet their needs, we discover the ability to share our own needs and they, too, can be met. This is part of a fulfilling life.

Besides having the attitude of a servant, we must also work toward unity. How do we get along with fellow believers when we do not agree with them on a theological or moral issue? It has been said that the most divisive group of people can be found within the walls of a church. What is our responsibility to others within our community of faith?

LEADER:
Choose the OPTION 1 Bible Study (below) or the OPTION 2 Study (page 42).

In Option 1, we will consider the example Jesus gave his disciples when he washed their feet (from John's Gospel). In our Option 2 Study (from the Book of Acts), we will consider Peter's visit with Cornelius, a fellow-believer, but a person with entirely different values than his own.

BIBLE STUDY / 30 Minutes / Groups of 4

Leader: Help the group choose an Option for study. Divide into groups of 4 for discussion. Remind the Leader for each foursome to move the group along so the Bible Study can be completed in the time allotted. Ask everyone to return together for the Caring Time for the final 15–45 minutes.

OPTION 1

Gospel Study / A Life of Service
John 13:2–17

STUDY

The following passage describes an event during the Last Supper (which Jesus celebrated with his disciples). Read John 13:2–17 and discuss the questions which follow with your group.

²The evening meal was being served, and the devil had already prompted Judas Iscariot, son of Simon, to betray Jesus. ³Jesus knew that the Father had put all things under his power, and that he had come from God and was returning to God; ⁴so he got up from the meal, took off his outer clothing, and wrapped a towel around his waist. ⁵After that, he poured water into a basin and began to wash his disciples' feet, drying them with the towel that was wrapped around him.

⁶He came to Simon Peter, who said to him, "Lord, are you going to wash my feet?"

⁷Jesus replied, "You do not realize now what I am doing, but later you will understand."

⁸"No," said Peter, "you shall never wash my feet."

Jesus answered, "Unless I wash you, you have no part with me."

⁹"Then, Lord," Simon Peter replied, "not just my feet but my hands and my head as well!"

¹⁰Jesus answered, "A person who has had a bath needs only to wash his feet; his whole body is clean. And you are clean, though not every one of you." ¹¹For he knew who was going to betray him, and that was why he said not every one was clean.

¹²When he had finished washing their feet, he put on his clothes and returned to his place. "Do you understand what I have done for you?" he asked them. ¹³"You call me 'Teacher' and 'Lord,' and rightly so, for that is what I am. ¹⁴Now that I, your Lord and Teacher, have washed your feet, you also should wash one another's feet. ¹⁵I have set you an example that you should do as I have done for you. ¹⁶I tell you the truth, no servant is greater than his master, nor is a messenger greater than the one who sent him. ¹⁷Now that you know these things, you will be blessed if you do them."

John 13:2–17, NIV

1. What do you think motivated Jesus to perform the act of footwashing at this point in time?
   ❑ The stench of dirty feet was ruining his supper.
   ❑ With everyone relaxed, it was a good time to teach them about servanthood before he died.
   ❑ He watched the disciples play power games among themselves.
   ❑ He wanted to show them his deep love for them.
   ❑ He wanted to give them a new model for their life together.

2. Why did Simon Peter initially refuse to let Jesus wash his feet?
   ❑ He thought one of the other disciples should do it.
   ❑ He didn't think he was worthy.
   ❑ He didn't want his hero to stoop to such lowly behavior.
   ❑ He thought it was too personal an act, and he felt embarrassed.
   ❑ He thought his feet were clean already.
   ❑ He didn't understand what Jesus was doing.

3. When Jesus told his disciples that they should wash one another's feet, he meant:
   - ❐ Their feet were so dirty they needed a second wash.
   - ❐ Footwashing should be observed regularly, like Communion.
   - ❐ They should be willing to do the lowliest tasks in service to others.
   - ❐ No one should do all the servant-tasks—they should share them.

4. When you were in the seventh grade, what kind of servant-tasks were you expected to do around the house?
   - ❐ make my bed
   - ❐ look after younger siblings
   - ❐ clean the dishes
   - ❐ yard work
   - ❐ take out the trash
   - ❐ all of them—both of my parents worked
   - ❐ clean my room
   - ❐ cook
   - ❐ laundry
   - ❐ vacuum
   - ❐ nothing

5. How did you feel about doing the tasks in question #4? What ingenious ways did you develop in order to avoid them?

6. What do you do for others right now which is most like "washing feet"—a somewhat unpleasant, humble servant-task? How do you feel about doing this?

7. Which of the following is true with relationship to your church involvement and servanthood?
   - ❐ My church involvement has nothing to do with serving—it's about showing up on Sunday morning.
   - ❐ My church involvement requires many servant-tasks, but most of them are pleasant.
   - ❐ My church involvement requires many servant-tasks, most of which are not pleasant.
   - ❐ The main pleasure I get from church comes from serving people.
   - ❐ I chose my church specifically so I wouldn't have to do unpleasant tasks like that.

8. What would it mean for you to take on the servant-mind of Christ in relation to your church involvement?
   - ❐ Sounds like I would have to choose something unpleasant.
   - ❐ I would have to change my attitude.
   - ❐ I would focus more on the needs of people than on showing up.
   - ❐ I would have to realize that self-fulfillment can only come if I am committed to serving others.
   - ❐ I would have to do a lot of things I'm not willing to do right now.

LEADER: When you have completed the Bible Study, move on to the Caring Time (page 45).

Epistle Study / Stretching Our Boundaries
Acts 10:9–23

STUDY

Read Acts 10:9–23 (and Leviticus 11:4–7,13–19 and 29–30 for background to this passage). Then discuss the questions which follow with your group. This is part of the story of Peter's vision and subsequent encounter with Cornelius.

⁹About noon the following day as they were on their journey and approaching the city, Peter went up on the roof to pray. ¹⁰He became hungry and wanted something to eat, and while the meal was being prepared, he fell into a trance. ¹¹He saw heaven opened and something like a large sheet being let down to earth by its four corners. ¹²It contained all kinds of four-footed animals, as well as reptiles of the earth and birds of the air. ¹³Then a voice told him, "Get up, Peter. Kill and eat."

¹⁴"Surely not, Lord!" Peter replied. "I have never eaten anything impure or unclean."

¹⁵The voice spoke to him a second time, "Do not call anything impure that God has made clean."

¹⁶This happened three times, and immediately the sheet was taken back to heaven.

¹⁷While Peter was wondering about the meaning of the vision, the men sent by Cornelius found out where Simon's house was and stopped at the gate. ¹⁸They called out, asking if Simon who was known as Peter was staying there.

¹⁹While Peter was still thinking about the vision, the Spirit said to him, "Simon, three men are looking for you. ²⁰So get up and go downstairs. Do not hesitate to go with them, for I have sent them."

²¹Peter went down and said to the men, "I'm the one you're looking for. Why have you come?"

²²The men replied, "We have come from Cornelius the centurion. He is a righteous and God-fearing man, who is respected by all the Jewish people. A holy angel told him to have you come to his house so that he could hear what you have to say." ²³Then Peter invited the men into the house to be his guests.

Acts 10:9–23, NIV

1. With these restrictions (in the Leviticus passage), how do you think Peter felt when he heard the voice order him to eat these animals?
   - ❐ I must have hit my head.
   - ❐ Peter, stay away from those anchovies.
   - ❐ God really can't be serious about this.
   - ❐ Is God trying to test me and my loyalty to him?
   - ❐ I know the rules—what's really going on here?

2. Growing up, what food did you refuse to eat?

3. Why was the command "to kill and eat" repeated three times?
   - ❐ Peter was hard of hearing.
   - ❐ Peter was a slow learner.
   - ❐ Peter just didn't get it.
   - ❐ other: _____

4. What do you think was Peter's response to verse 15: "Do not call anything impure that God has made clean"?
   - ❐ But God said before that these things were impure.
   - ❐ Why is God changing the rules in midstream?
   - ❐ I can't believe that this is God talking.
   - ❐ I need to go see a doctor—I'm hearing and seeing things.
   - ❐ other: _____

5. What are some beliefs you have held that have limited your ability to reach out to fellow believers who are "different" from you?
   - ❐ my view of Scripture
   - ❐ my view of the role of women in the church
   - ❐ my view of abortion
   - ❐ my view of homosexuality
   - ❐ my view of the use of public monies
   - ❐ my view of tax dollars supporting the arts
   - ❐ other: _____

6. In light of this passage, how would God feel if you moved beyond these limits?
   - ❐ He doesn't want me to associate with people who don't hold the same views I do.
   - ❐ He would be pleased that I could look beyond the differences of opinion to our common faith.
   - ❐ He wants me to try to persuade others of my personal "right" way of thinking.
   - ❐ other: _____

"Love is always open arms. If you close your arms about love you will find that you are left holding only yourself."
—Leo Buscaglia

7. What new relationships has God given you recently?
   ❏ people who have moved into the neighborhood
   ❏ new coworkers
   ❏ a new family in church
   ❏ a new relative through a recent marriage
   ❏ some friends I have made
   ❏ other: _____

8. How has God brought these people into your life? How have you influenced each other?

9. Who are you most likely to speak against or judge?
   ❏ liberals   ❏ conservatives
   ❏ people of another race   ❏ illegal immigrants
   ❏ wealthy people   ❏ welfare families
   ❏ Democrats/Republicans   ❏ alcoholics and drug addicts
   ❏ young people   ❏ old people
   ❏ people of another faith   ❏ other: _____

LEADER: When you have completed the Bible Study, move on to the Caring Time (page 45).

10. How does this passage challenge you to change your way of relating to the group (or groups) you checked in question #9?

COMMENT

What has happened to our unity? Denominations now number in the hundreds. Even the restrictive ranks of Evangelicalism are divided into more than 30 groups. And each group confesses a common faith in the Lord Jesus Christ. Denominational lines and religious labels are drawn tightly. Ask 50 persons from the street if they are Christians. Chances are good that they would not identify themselves as Christians or non-Christians, but as Methodists or Presbyterians or Baptists. So much for our unity. The unity Christ desires is one that strengthens and encourages us on our pilgrimage. In fact, when that type of unity is present, we begin to walk in such confidence that there's a definite hint of invincibility in our faith.

CARING TIME / 15–45 Minutes / All Together

Leader: Bring all of the foursomes back together for a time of caring and affirmation. Upon completion of the affirmation time, spend time together in prayer.

AFFIRMATION

Pass the Blessing, Please. You have probably been richly blessed by the people in your small group. Now is the time to tell them how they have blessed you.

You can use this heart-warmer in two different ways. First, you can go around your circle and take turns telling the person on your right or left how they have blessed your life. Or you can go around the circle and take turns letting each group member tell each person how they have felt blessed by them. The second option might be a good choice for a group that is ending a covenant (or ending their group completely).

- ❐ You have blessed me recently when you told the story about ...
- ❐ What inspires me most about your character is ...
- ❐ The aspect of your personality I would like to emulate in my life is ...
- ❐ You have a way with people that I admire very much ...
- ❐ There is something about your faith in God that I really like ...
- ❐ I would use three of the following words to describe you because you are ...

accepting	active	adventurous
aware	confident	considerate
creative	encouraging	good-hearted
helpful	authentic	honest
influential	inspiring	loyal
open	productive	real
righteous	risk-taking	sensitive
spontaneous	supportive	thoughtful
tolerant	vulnerable	warm

PRAYER

Take a moment to share prayer requests. Then pray for the requests of other group members. If you are uncomfortable praying aloud, pray silently and conclude by saying "Amen" so the next person will know to continue.

ACTION

1. Identify two servant-tasks you can do in your church. Make plans to do them this week.

2. Identify a way you can cross a "boundary" with another believer.

SESSION 6
Loving Others: Outside the Community of Faith

PURPOSE

To discover ways to strengthen relationships with people outside the community of faith.

AGENDA

 Gathering   Bible Study   Caring Time

OPEN

 GATHERING / 15 Minutes / All Together

Leader: Read the instructions for Step One and go first. Then read the Introduction (Step 2) and explain the choices for Bible Study.

Step One: You Remind Me Of ... Write your name on a slip of paper and put it in a hat. Let everyone in the group select a name from the hat, but don't tell anyone whose name you have drawn. Choose a national park or monument that best describes the person you have selected. When everyone is finished, read out loud what you chose and see if the group can guess who you are describing.

GRAND CANYON NATIONAL PARK: What an impressive vista! You have character that has taken years of patience and constant attention.

GOLDEN GATE NATIONAL PARK: You bring people together and bridge the gap in a beautiful, stunning way.

SEQUOIA NATIONAL PARK: Your growth is so impressive that you reach into the skies and provide shade and security for many.

YOSEMITE NATIONAL PARK: You are the most popular choice for an exciting and adventurous experience!

MAMMOTH CAVE NATIONAL PARK: With miles of underground passageways, you epitomize depth, mystery and hidden treasures.

STATUE OF LIBERTY NATIONAL MONUMENT: You are a living symbol to those around you of freedom, hope and a new life.

MOUNT RUSHMORE: You are an enduring testimony to leadership, character and integrity.

YELLOWSTONE NATIONAL PARK: With your hot springs and geysers, you are a source of warmth for those who get close to you.

MOUNT RAINIER NATIONAL PARK: You keep people looking up, and your high standards can be seen from a great distance.

INTRODUCTION

Step Two: Loving Others: Outside the Community of Faith. In our previous session, we discussed the ways to strengthen our relationships with fellow believers. We discovered that through servanthood and pursuing unity (despite our diversity), our relationships can be made stronger. But what do we do with people who are outside the community of faith? We are not talking about those who hold a different view of a fine theological point, or even those who disagree with us politically. We are now looking at people who are not believers. We are talking about people we would not normally associate with. We may not associate with them because we grew up believing that we shouldn't associate with them. Depending on the area of the country we live in, these may be people who might even be Christians, but of a different faith.

The point is Jesus went out of his way to associate with people that the rest of society had considered to be outcasts. They may have been outcasts because of their low social standing, or because they had a particular disease or illness, or maybe because they were from a different country. Often we don't associate with certain people because of our prejudices and stereotyping (and not because we have personally met them and didn't get along with them).

LEADER:
Choose the
OPTION 1 Bible
Study (below)
or the OPTION 2
Study (page 51).

Scripture has much to say about relating to and loving people outside the community of faith, and we will look at some of that teaching in this session. In Option 1 (from John's Gospel), we will consider what Jesus has to say about breaking down cultural barriers. In Option 2 (from Paul's letter to the Romans), we will consider his teaching about loving those outside of our faith.

BIBLE STUDY / 30 Minutes / Groups of 4

Leader: Help the group choose an Option for study. Divide into groups of 4 for discussion. Remind the Leader for each foursome to move the group along so the Bible Study can be completed in the time allotted. Ask everyone to return together for the Caring Time for the final 15–45 minutes.

OPTION 1

Gospel Study / Breaking Barriers
John 4:4–26

STUDY

Jesus crosses the boundary from the Jews into the world of the Samaritans. By doing so, he reveals God's love for all kinds of people. Read John 4:4–26 and discuss your responses to the following questions with the group.

⁴Now he had to go through Samaria. ⁵So he came to a town in Samaria called Sychar, near the plot of ground Jacob had given to his son Joseph. ⁶Jacob's well was there, and Jesus, tired as he was from the journey, sat down by the well. It was about the sixth hour.

⁷When a Samaritan woman came to draw water, Jesus said to her, "Will you give me a drink?" ⁸(His disciples had gone into the town to buy food.)

⁹The Samaritan woman said to him, "You are a Jew and I am a Samaritan woman. How can you ask me for a drink?" (For Jews do not associate with Samaritans.)

¹⁰Jesus answered her, "If you knew the gift of God and who it is that asks you for a drink, you would have asked him and he would have given you living water."

¹¹"Sir," the woman said, "you have nothing to draw with and the well is deep. Where can you get this living water? ¹²Are you greater than our father Jacob, who gave us the well and drank from it himself, as did also his sons and his flocks and herds?"

¹³Jesus answered, "Everyone who drinks this water will be thirsty again, ¹⁴but whoever drinks the water I give him will never thirst. Indeed, the water I give him will become in him a spring of water welling up to eternal life."

¹⁵The woman said to him, "Sir, give me this water so that I won't get thirsty and have to keep coming here to draw water."

¹⁶He told her, "Go, call your husband and come back."

¹⁷"I have no husband," she replied.

Jesus said to her, "You are right when you say you have no husband. ¹⁸The fact is, you have had five husbands, and the man you now have is not your husband. What you have just said is quite true."

¹⁹"Sir," the woman said, "I can see that you are a prophet. ²⁰Our fathers worshiped on this mountain, but you Jews claim that the place where we must worship is in Jerusalem."

²¹Jesus declared, "Believe me, woman, a time is coming when you will worship the Father neither on this mountain nor in Jerusalem. ²²You Samaritans worship what you do not know; we worship what we do know, for salvation is from the Jews. ²³Yet a time is coming and has now come when the true worshipers will worship the Father in spirit and truth, for they are the kind of worshipers the Father seeks. ²⁴God is spirit, and his worshipers must worship in spirit and in truth."

²⁵The woman said, "I know that Messiah" (called Christ) "is coming. When he comes, he will explain everything to us."

²⁶Then Jesus declared, "I who speak to you am he."

John 4:4–26, NIV

1. Imagine that you are a reporter for *The Sychar Sentinel* (where every day is a slow news day), and you had heard of this incident by the well. What headline would you use to report it?
   - ❏ "Rabbi Has Rendezvous With Local Woman at Jacob's Well"
   - ❏ "Scandal Sizzles in Sychar! Will Rabbi Wed Five-Time Loser?"
   - ❏ "Local Woman Claims Messiah Visited Sychar—Experts Scoff"
   - ❏ "Irreputable Woman Claims Life-Changing Encounter With Rabbi"

2. As someone who was taught from birth to despise Samaritans, how would you feel when Jesus decided to go through Samaria instead of taking the long way home?
   - ❏ I would have insisted that we take the longer route.
   - ❏ I would have been upset at Jesus for going against his Jewish upbringing.
   - ❏ I would have been afraid.
   - ❏ I would have been excited about challenging the status quo.
   - ❏ I would have been looking over my shoulder the whole time.

3. Jews did not associate with Samaritans. When you were growing up, what kind of people were you warned not to associate with?
   - ❏ people of a different race
   - ❏ kids who used foul language
   - ❏ foreigners
   - ❏ people of another religion
   - ❏ people from "the other side of the tracks"
   - ❏ people of a different political persuasion
   - ❏ We could associate with anyone.

4. What does this story say to you about breaking down the barriers that exist between races, cultures, and other groups?
   - ❏ It starts with talking and listening.
   - ❏ It starts with not worrying about what others tell you about people and learning for yourself.
   - ❏ It comes from realizing we all "thirst" for the same things in life.
   - ❏ It will happen when we follow Christ's example.
   - ❏ other: _____

5. "Nice" girls didn't come to the well at noontime ("the sixth hour"). Why did Jesus risk his reputation to ask a favor of this woman?
   - ❏ He wanted to challenge the status quo.
   - ❏ He was thirsty and couldn't get a drink for himself.
   - ❏ He wanted to see what she would do.
   - ❏ Reputation didn't matter as much to him as loving people who are in need.
   - ❏ other: _____

"We are born helpless. As soon as we are fully conscious we discover loneliness. We need others physically, emotionally, intellectually. We need them if we are to know anything, even ourselves."
—C. S. Lewis

"To reconcile man with man and not with God is to reconcile no one at all."
—Thomas Merton

LEADER: When you have completed the Bible Study, move on to the Caring Time (page 54).

6. What was the woman's response when Jesus said, "If you knew the gift of God and who it is that asks you for a drink, you would have asked him and he would have given you living water"?
   ❏ She was stumbling for an answer at first.
   ❏ A spiritual desire for something was aroused in her.
   ❏ Curiosity—"Is it possible this is the thing I've been looking for?"
   ❏ Skepticism—"Who do you think you are?"
   ❏ other: _____

7. Jesus offered this woman "living water" for what she was thirsting for in life. What do you think she really wanted?
   ❏ a relationship with a truly caring man
   ❏ acceptance of who she was
   ❏ forgiveness for the life she had led
   ❏ fellowship with God
   ❏ other: _____

8. What are you thirsting for most in life right now?
   ❏ acceptance of who I am
   ❏ a sense of meaning in life
   ❏ some genuine friendships
   ❏ fellowship with God
   ❏ other: _____

9. What do you need to do to relieve your thirst?
   ❏ accept the forgiveness that Jesus offers
   ❏ seek Jesus' direction in my life
   ❏ reach out to people like Jesus did, especially past those religious barriers
   ❏ practice more spiritual discipline—in private Bible study and prayer
   ❏ other: _____

Epistle Study / Loving Outsiders
Romans 12:9–21

In this section of Paul's letter to the Romans, he describes relationships between Christians. Then he concludes this section by discussing (in verses 14–21) the question of how to relate to those who aren't Christians. Read Romans 12:9–21 and discuss your responses to the following questions with your group.

⁹Love must be sincere. Hate what is evil; cling to what is good. ¹⁰Be devoted to one another in brotherly love. Honor one another above yourselves. ¹¹Never be lacking in zeal, but keep your spiritual fervor, serving the Lord. ¹²Be joyful in hope, patient in affliction, faithful in prayer. ¹³Share with God's people who are in need. Practice hospitality.

¹⁴Bless those who persecute you; bless and do not curse. ¹⁵Rejoice with those who rejoice; mourn with those who mourn. ¹⁶Live in harmony with one another. Do not be proud, but be willing to associate with people in low position. Do not be conceited.

¹⁷Do not repay anyone evil for evil. Be careful to do what is right in the eyes of everybody. ¹⁸If it is possible, as far as it depends on you, live at peace with everyone. ¹⁹Do not take revenge, my friends, but leave room for God's wrath, for it is written: "It is mine to avenge; I will repay," says the Lord. ²⁰On the contrary:

> *"If your enemy is hungry feed him;*
> *if he is thirsty, give him something to drink.*
> *In doing this, you will heap burning coals on his head."*

²¹Do not be overcome by evil, but overcome evil with good.

Romans 12:9–21, NIV

1. Imagine that you were in the congregation at Rome hearing Paul's letter for the first time. What would be your initial reaction?
   ❒ Easy for him to say—he doesn't have Rome breathing down his neck.
   ❒ What fairy-tale world did you say this guy stepped out of?
   ❒ This is good advice—hard to follow, but good.
   ❒ This is the key we need to turn our world around.

2. What do you think Paul's motivation was for including this passage in the letter?
- ❐ He wanted to frustrate struggling Christians with these impossible standards.
- ❐ He wanted to give the people a New Testament version of the Ten Commandments.
- ❐ He wanted to help Christians deal with a hostile world.
- ❐ He wanted to give people a moral target at which to aim.
- ❐ other: _____

3. Which of the following instructions (about responding to non-Christians) do you think is the most effective as you deal with them?
- ❐ We must offer a blessing in the face of hostility.
- ❐ When our enemies experience joy or success, we must enter wholeheartedly into their rejoicing and not begrudge them this joy (because they mistreated us before).
- ❐ We are to do all we can to promote peace and harmony.
- ❐ We shouldn't be haughty in our response: "You can't hurt me. I'm better than you."
- ❐ We are not to find someone lower than ourselves to lord it over.
- ❐ Revenge and wrath must be left to God.
- ❐ We must respond to an enemy in need with acts of love.
- ❐ We dare not choose the way of evil in order to fight evil.

4. Paul says we are to "do what is right in the eyes of everybody." When you were a child in grade school, whose approval did you seek by doing what was right?
- ❐ my mother
- ❐ my father
- ❐ a grandmother
- ❐ a grandfather
- ❐ a teacher
- ❐ a minister
- ❐ my friends
- ❐ myself
- ❐ God
- ❐ other: _____

5. Rate your present performance in each of the moral directions (related to loving others) which Paul gives us in this passage:

LOVING SINCERELY:

1	2	3	4	5	6	7	8	9	10
a total wipeout				struggling					on target

HONORING OTHERS ABOVE MYSELF:

1	2	3	4	5	6	7	8	9	10
a total wipeout				struggling					on target

SHARING WITH GOD'S PEOPLE IN NEED:

1	2	3	4	5	6	7	8	9	10
a total wipeout				struggling					on target

PRACTICING HOSPITALITY TO STRANGERS:

1	2	3	4	5	6	7	8	9	10
a total wipeout				struggling					on target

BLESSING THOSE WHO PERSECUTE ME:

1	2	3	4	5	6	7	8	9	10
a total wipeout				struggling					on target

REJOICING WITH THOSE WHO REJOICE:

1	2	3	4	5	6	7	8	9	10
a total wipeout				struggling					on target

MOURNING WITH THOSE WHO MOURN:

1	2	3	4	5	6	7	8	9	10
a total wipeout				struggling					on target

LIVING IN HARMONY WITH OTHERS:

1	2	3	4	5	6	7	8	9	10
a total wipeout				struggling					on target

WILLING TO ASSOCIATE WITH PEOPLE OF LOW POSITION:

1	2	3	4	5	6	7	8	9	10
a total wipeout				struggling					on target

NOT REPAYING EVIL FOR EVIL:

1	2	3	4	5	6	7	8	9	10
a total wipeout				struggling					on target

LEADER: When you have completed the Bible Study, move on to the Caring Time (page 54).

6. How will you seek to apply this passage to your life?
   ❏ remember how God has loved and forgiven me
   ❏ admit to myself how far I'm falling short in my efforts to love other people
   ❏ ask God for his power to love in this way
   ❏ be a continuing part of a community that encourages this kind of loving
   ❏ other: _____

CARING TIME / 15–45 Minutes/All Together

Leader: Bring all of the foursomes back together for a time of Caring support for each other using the Sharing, Prayer and Action sections below.

SHARING

My Small Group Is ... How would you describe your small group? Choose one of the images below which best describes your small group. Then go around your group and tell them why you chose the one you did:

AN ORCHARD: Whenever I'm in this group, I feel like a fragrant and healthy apple tree, because of all the growing I've done and all of the fruit I've been able to share.

A TEEPEE: We couldn't stand tall and provide warmth and shelter if we didn't lean on each other.

A BIRD'S NEST: I know how a baby bird feels, because being part of this group makes me feel nurtured and protected.

A THINK TANK: This group must be full of geniuses! We seem to be able to understand every issue and work out every problem with creativity and discernment.

THE 12 MUSKETEERS: It's "all for one and one for all" with this group. I always feel like I belong, and that I'm part of a great team.

THE BRADY BUNCH: I feel like I'm part of one big, happy family. We're not perfect, but we love and accept each other.

AN OASIS: While the rest of the world can be so harsh and unforgiving, this group is a refreshing stop on the journey of life.

A LITTER OF PUPPIES: You are a fun, friendly and enthusiastic bundle of joy. I feel younger every time we get together.

A M*A*S*H* UNIT: This group is like a field hospital. I came in wounded, and now I feel so much better—I have a bunch of new friends to boot!

PRAYER

If someone is still uncomfortable praying aloud, encourage them to pray silently. When they conclude their prayer, ask them to say "Amen" so the next person will know to continue.

ACTION

Choose one non-Christian person you know. Plan two things you can do for that person this week to demonstrate God's love.

SESSION 7
Loving Our Enemies

PURPOSE | To develop a healthy and Biblical view of loving our enemies.

AGENDA |  **Gathering**   **Bible Study**   **Caring Time**

OPEN | ## GATHERING / 15 Minutes / All Together

Leader: This is the final session together. You may want to have your Caring Time first. If not, be sure to allow a full 25 minutes at the end of the session.

Step One: Who's It Gonna Be? Write down the name of a friend you would choose to join you in the following activities. Why would you choose this person? You can also play this game by choosing which family member or relative you would choose to do these activities with:

_____ GO FISHING: a wonderful, peaceful afternoon by the water, talking softly and bragging about "the big one that got away."

_____ PRAY: an activity to be shared with someone with a deep faith and a trustful heart.

_____ GO SHOPPING: it's fun to walk around with a friend and look into store windows and buy the perfect item. This is going to be a busy day, so put on your walking shoes!

_____ GET STUCK ON A DESERTED ISLAND: for an adventure like this, you'll need someone who is crafty and resourceful, a great companion and easy to get along with.

_____ EAT SUSHI: who would you choose to go eat something new and different? If not sushi, try Rocky Mountain oysters, pig knuckles or calf sweetbreads.

_____ TALK ABOUT MY PROBLEMS: a task like this requires someone who is sympathetic, compassionate and understanding. You do not want someone who will pass judgment, but will listen intently.

_____ CRY WITH: when you're most vulnerable, you need a special companion who is nurturing and protective.

_____ GO TO DISNEYLAND: it's a great trip to a giant playground; you'll want to take someone who is fun, childlike and daring.

_____ TALK ABOUT GOD: when discussing deep spiritual truths, you want to talk with someone who has an accurate and positive understanding of God.

INTRODUCTION

Step Two: Loving Our Enemies. Will Rogers once said, "I never met a man I didn't like." Many of us would reply, "Evidently, Will never met so-and-so." If we are honest with ourselves, there are people in our lives with whom we can't get along and whom we don't like. However, we are taught in Scripture to love all people, including our enemies.

The thought of loving someone who divorced us, cut us out of a business deal, told rumors about us, or hurt us in some way seems beyond our abilities. But to "love" a murderer or a person who leads a warring faction seems ludicrous. What does the Bible really say about loving our enemies, unconditional love and cooperation?

This may be the most difficult area of relationships for us to work on. It's bad enough that we have to admit we have enemies. But the idea of working with them and building relationships with them may be beyond what we can realistically deal with on a daily basis.

Steve Covey in his book *The Seven Habits of Highly Effective People* talks about ways to negotiate and ways to cooperate with others, so that both parties win. The principle of Win/Win is fundamental to success in all of our interactions, and it embraces five interdependent dimensions of life. It begins with character and moves toward relationships, out of which flow agreements. It is nurtured in an environment where structure and systems are based on Win/Win; and it involves process.

LEADER:
Choose the
OPTION 1 Bible
Study (page 57)
or the OPTION 2
Study (page 59).

In the Option 1 Study (from Matthew's Gospel), Jesus teaches us what it means to truly love our enemies. And in the Option 2 Study (from Paul's letter to the Philippians), we will discover Paul's teaching on unconditional love, which he learned in prison.

 # BIBLE STUDY / 25 Minutes / Groups of 4

Leader: Remind the Leaders to end their Bible Study time five minutes earlier than usual to allow ample time for your final Caring Time—deciding what the group will do next.

Gospel Study / Some People
Matthew 5:38–48

STUDY

Jesus totally rejects the thought of personal revenge, and calls instead for non-retaliation. Read Matthew 5:38–48 and discuss your responses to the following questions with your group.

38"You have heard that it was said, 'Eye for eye, and tooth for tooth.' 39But I tell you, Do not resist an evil person. If someone strikes you on the right cheek, turn to him the other also. 40And if someone wants to sue you and take your tunic, let him have your cloak as well. 41If someone forces you to go one mile, go with him two miles. 42Give to the one who asks you, and do not turn away from the one who wants to borrow from you.

43"You have heard that it was said, 'Love your neighbor and hate your enemy.' 44But I tell you: Love your enemies and pray for those who perse-cute you, 45that you may be sons of your Father in heaven. He causes his sun to rise on the evil and the good, and sends rain on the righteous and the unrighteous. 46If you love those who love you, what reward will you get? Are not even the tax collectors doing that? 47And if you greet only your brothers, what are you doing more than others? Do not even pagans do that? 48Be perfect, therefore, as your heavenly Father is perfect."

Matthew 5:38–48, NIV

1. Finish this sentence: "If Christians were to take this passage seri-ously, it would ..."
    ❒ put all of the lawyers out of business.
    ❒ put the banks and lending institutions out of business.
    ❒ get us all in better physical shape by going the extra mile.
    ❒ allow crime to run rampant.
    ❒ make us crazy by trying to be perfect.
    ❒ change lives like no rehabilitation program ever has before.
    ❒ make the world a safer and more peaceful place.

2. In this passage, Jesus gives standards of conduct for life which ...
    ❒ I will never achieve.
    ❒ I want to strive toward.
    ❒ I must attain before I can receive God's mercy.
    ❒ aren't standards, but are simply moral ideals.
    ❒ are perspectives I should develop as a recipient of God's mercy.
    ❒ other: _____

3. On the following moral issues, put an "**X**" on the scale according to which position is closest to yours:

ON REVENGE:

_____
call in "Rambo"   immediately forgive and forget

ON CRIME:

_____
call in "Dirty Harry"   change lives through love and opportunity

ON LAWSUITS:

_____
sue their socks off   we can settle things if we just talk

4. How did your parents resolve conflicts between you and your sibling or friend?
   - ❑ let us fight it out
   - ❑ prayed about it
   - ❑ yelled at us
   - ❑ ignored it
   - ❑ had us sit down to talk about it
   - ❑ took sides
   - ❑ sent us out of the house
   - ❑ They really didn't care.

5. When you're in conflict, which relationship is the hardest for you to reconcile?
   - ❑ my spouse
   - ❑ my parents
   - ❑ my neighbors
   - ❑ my professional peers
   - ❑ my enemies
   - ❑ my children—especially my teenager(s)
   - ❑ my friends—especially my close friends
   - ❑ other: _____

6. Which of these "enemies" would you have a hard time loving?
   - ❑ my ex-spouse
   - ❑ anyone from the IRS
   - ❑ my spouse's ex-spouse
   - ❑ those I fought in war
   - ❑ persons of a different race
   - ❑ a rival at work
   - ❑ liberals
   - ❑ conservatives
   - ❑ other: _____

"Returning hate for hate multiplies hate, adding deeper darkness to a night already devoid of stars."
—Martin Luther King, Jr.

58

7. Think of someone who has hurt you in the past. In light of verses 43–48, what would your response be if he/she walked into the room right now?
- ❑ I would get up and leave.
- ❑ I would seek revenge—maybe even physical harm.
- ❑ I would remind them how they hurt me.
- ❑ I would forgive and forget.

8. Identify an area in your life where you need to "turn the other cheek."

LEADER: When you have completed the Bible Study, move on to the Caring Time (page 62).

9. When you leave this session today, how will you respond to the radical demands of this passage?
- ❑ conveniently forget it, like I've always done before
- ❑ struggle with it, but in the end stay with my relational patterns
- ❑ make some changes, but perhaps not all that this demands
- ❑ shoot for it all—turn my life around with unconditional love

COMMENT

In a world which focuses and thrives on competition, Jesus' words are a stark contrast. The world lives by a Win/Lose paradigm. But Jesus calls us to a Win/Win way of life. We are called to cooperate with our friends and family, and try to get along with our enemies. After all, even the world is nice to people they like. But a child of God is called to love his or her enemies.

OPTION 2

Epistle Study / Paul's Enemies
Philippians 1:12–18a, 27–2:4

STUDY

In his letter to the Philippians, Paul points to two positive results from his imprisonment: (1) The Gospel is being heard and recognized by all sorts of people, who might otherwise not have heard it or noticed it (v. 13); and (2) others in Rome have been encouraged to preach even more (vv. 14–18). Read Philippians 1:12–18a, 27–2:4 and discuss your responses to the following questions with your group.

12Now I want you to know, brothers, that what has happened to me has really served to advance the gospel. 13As a result, it has become clear throughout the whole palace guard and to everyone else that I am in chains for Christ. 14Because of my chains, most of the brothers in the Lord have been encouraged to speak the word of God more courageously and fearlessly.

[15]It is true that some preach Christ out of envy and rivalry, but others out of goodwill. [16]The latter do so in love, knowing that I am put here for the defense of the gospel. [17]The former preach Christ out of selfish ambition, not sincerely, supposing that they can stir up trouble for me while I am in chains. [18]But what does it matter? The important thing is that in every way, whether from false motives or true, Christ is preached. And because of this I rejoice. ...

[27]Whatever happens, conduct yourselves in a manner worthy of the gospel of Christ. Then, whether I come and see you or only hear about you in my absence, I will know that you stand firm in one spirit, contending as one man for the faith of the gospel [28]without being frightened in any way by those who oppose you. This is a sign to them that they will be destroyed, but that you will be saved—and that by God. [29]For it has been granted to you on behalf of Christ not only to believe on him, but also to suffer for him, [30]since you are going through the same struggle you saw I had, and now hear that I still have.

2 *If you have any encouragement from being united with Christ, if any comfort from his love, if any fellowship with the Spirit, if any tenderness and compassion, [2]then make my joy complete by being like-minded, having the same love, being one in spirit and purpose. [3]Do nothing out of selfish ambition or vain conceit, but in humility consider others better than yourselves. [4]Each of you should look not only to your own interests, but also to the interests of others.*

Philippians 1:12–18a, 27–2:4, NIV

1. Imagine that you are a member of the Philippian church and you have just heard Paul's letter for the first time. What would your initial reaction be?
   - ❒ that house imprisonment must be getting to Paul's head
   - ❒ I wish we had a sense of community like Paul is talking about.
   - ❒ Paul must be living in some dream world—not the real world.
   - ❒ I wish so-and-so could hear this letter.

2. Paul is imprisoned because of his stand for the Gospel. His imprisonment has spurred others to preach the Gospel courageously and fearlessly. What is your view in difficult situations?
   - ❒ Like Paul, I tend to see God's hand in my difficult circumstances.
   - ❒ I occasionally see God's hand in my difficult circumstances.
   - ❒ I think Satan is responsible for difficulties in my life.
   - ❒ Difficult circumstances strengthen my faith.
   - ❒ Difficult circumstances are a sign of unconfessed sin in my life.
   - ❒ Difficult circumstances are a sign that I am doing God's will.
   - ❒ When I see others suffering for the sake of the Gospel, I am encouraged.
   - ❒ When I see others suffering for the sake of the Gospel, I get discouraged and think, "What's the use?"

3. Paul was imprisoned because of his love for God and God's children. What similar sacrifice has someone (besides Christ) made for you in order to show you love?
   ❐ my mother, who stayed up all night when I was ill
   ❐ my parents, who worked extra hours for money to send me to college
   ❐ Martin Luther King and others, who suffered and went to prison for racial freedom
   ❐ army buddies, who endangered themselves to cover for me
   ❐ I don't remember anyone who did such a thing for me.

4. Below are some of the teachings of this passage which have a bearing on community. Using this scale (1= totally disagree to 10= totally agree), assign a number to each which reflects the degree to which you disagree or agree with them:

1	2	3	4	5	6	7	8	9	10
totally disagree				somewhat agree					totally agree

   ___ We will suffer as people of faith.
   ___ Some have wrong motives in sharing the Gospel, but that's okay.
   ___ We are encouraged when we are united with Christ.
   ___ We are comforted by God's love.
   ___ We are to be of the same spirit, love and purpose.
   ___ The more we're of "the same mind," the more harmoniously we will live.
   ___ We are to be as concerned for the interests of others as our own interests.
   ___ The road to unity is by the path of humble sacrifice.

5. Which of the actions described in this letter do you think is most important in building a supportive Christian community?
   ❐ people taking on the work that others can no longer do (1:14)
   ❐ rejoicing in the accomplishments of others (1:18)
   ❐ a unity of spirit and direction (1:27 and 2:2)
   ❐ lack of the competition that comes with ambition and pride (2:3)
   ❐ looking after each other's interests (2:4)

6. Paul talks about community coming (in part) from the fact that his readers were going through the same struggle they had seen him go through (1:30). When have you found community in knowing someone else was experiencing the same struggle you were going through?

"Taking the Gospel to people wherever they are—death row, the ghetto, or next door—is frontline evangelism. It is our one hope for breaking down barriers and for restoring the sense of community, of caring for one another, that our decadent, impersonalized culture has sucked out of us."
—Charles Colson

7. Since churches often divide along denominational, cultural, theological and social lines, what would it mean to apply verse 27 in your community in concrete ways? What would have to change in you to make such unity possible?

8. Who do you have the hardest time being "one in spirit and purpose" with (2:2)?
   - ❐ my spouse
   - ❐ my children
   - ❐ a leader in the church
   - ❐ my parents
   - ❐ my boss
   - ❐ other: _____

9. Which of the things Paul talks about would help you relate to this person better?
   - ❐ stop being frightened by him or her (1:28)
   - ❐ show him or her more "tenderness and compassion" (2:1)
   - ❐ forget some of my selfish ambitions (2:3)
   - ❐ give greater consideration to his or her interests and needs (2:4)
   - ❐ see our unity in Christ (2:1)

LEADER: When you have completed the Bible Study, move on to the Caring Time (below).

CARING TIME / 15–45 Minutes / All Together

Leader: This is decision time. These four steps are designed to help you evaluate your group experience and to decide about the future.

EVALUATION

Take a few minutes to review your experience and reflect. Go around on each point and finish the sentences:

1. What are some specific things you have learned about how to build relationships in your life?

2. Are you thinking or acting any differently because of your involvement in this study? In what way?

3. As I see it, our purpose and goal as a group was to:

4. We achieved our goal(s):
   - ❐ completely
   - ❐ almost completely
   - ❐ somewhat
   - ❐ We blew it.

5. The high point in this course for me has been:
   - ❐ the Scripture exercises
   - ❐ the sharing
   - ❐ discovering myself
   - ❐ belonging to a real community
   - ❐ the fun of the fellowship
   - ❐ finding new life/purpose for my life

6. One of the most significant things I learned was ...

7. In my opinion, our group functioned:
   - ❐ smoothly, and we grew
   - ❐ pretty well, but we didn't grow
   - ❐ It was tough, but we grew.
   - ❐ It was tough, and we didn't grow.

8. The thing I appreciate most about the group as a whole is:

CONTINUATION

Do you want to continue as a group? If so, what do you need to improve? Finish the sentence:

*"If I were to suggest one thing we could work on as a group,
it would be ..."*

MAKE A COVENANT

A covenant is a promise made to each other in the presence of God. Its purpose is to indicate your intention to make yourselves available to one another for the fulfillment of the purposes you share. In a spirit of prayer, work your way through the following sentences, trying to reach an agreement on each statement pertaining to your ongoing life together. Write out your covenant like a contract, stating your purpose, goals and the ground rules for your group.

1. The purpose of our group will be ... (finish the sentence)

2. Our goals will be ...

3. We will meet for _____ weeks, after which we will decide if we wish to continue as a group.

4. We will meet from _____ to _____ and we will strive to start on time and end on time.

5. We will meet at _____ (place) or we will rotate from house to house.

6. We will agree to the following ground rules for our group (check):

☐ PRIORITY: While you are in the course, you give the group meetings priority.

☐ PARTICIPATION: Everyone participates and no one dominates.

☐ RESPECT: Everyone is given the right to their own opinion, and all questions are encouraged and respected.

☐ CONFIDENTIALITY: Anything that is said in the meeting is never repeated outside the meeting.

☐ EMPTY CHAIR: The group stays open to new people at every meeting, as long as they understand the ground rules.

☐ SUPPORT: Permission is given to call upon each other in time of need at any time.

☐ ACCOUNTABILITY: We agree to let the members of the group hold us accountable to the commitments which each of us make in whatever loving ways we decide upon.

CURRICULUM

If you decide to continue as a group for a few more weeks, what are you going to use for study and discipline? There are 15 other studies available at this 201 Series level. 301 Courses, designed for deeper Bible Study with Study Notes, are also available.

For more information about small group resources and possible directions, please contact your small group coordinator or SERENDIPITY at 1-800-525-9563 or visit us at: www.serendipityhouse.com.